Grow You Own Vegetables

Rachelle Strauss

Foreword by Heather Gorringe, CEO, Wiggly Wigglers

**FLAME TREE
PUBLISHING**

Contents

There are so many reasons to grow your own vegetables that if you are not already a convert you will be after reading this book! Growing your own food can save you money; it can help protect the environment, from reduced food miles to seasonal and organic growing; it can reduce food and packaging waste; it is great for your health and wellbeing in a plethora of ways; and it can be invaluable getting the kids involved.

This section will reveal that you can grow veg pretty much anywhere – the first thing you have to do is consider what you have to work with: how much space do you have? what type of soil do you have? do you have a patio, balcony or window sill that could work instead of a garden? what are the light conditions? do you have space for a greenhouse? Is it worth looking for an allotment to rent? Then you can start to design your vegetable plot.

Once you know where you are going to plant your
vegetables you need to decide what you will plant. You
will be spoilt for choice but must make logical decisions.
What are your tastes and dietary needs? What you grow
will depend on the meals you intend to make and who
you have to make them for. The choice will also depend
on the conditions of the plot and your time and energy –
some plants will only grow in full sun, and some take less
work than others.

This section gives more advice on
planning your plot. Then it's time to get
down and dirty and prepare the ground and
feed the soil. Tips are given on
making your own compost and how to
use it. Making a raised bed may be the
solution – find out how. Or if you have no
garden, here's how to get started with
containers. Everything you need to know
about seeds, fertilizers and tools is
provided so that you will be ready to
start growing!

How To Grow 120

Now to plant those seeds! Learn how to prepare the soil for sowing, when and how to sow – as well as sowing indoors and outdoors and how to transplant your seedlings. Learn the basics of how to tend and care for your seedlings and plants, from feeding to watering. Discover the benefits of organic growing and how to be successful at it. Tips on how to extend the growing season are also included.

Reaping The Rewards. . . 140

Now for the exciting moment of harvesting your hard-earned crop. Get the most out of your produce by planning your harvest well, and learn how and when in general to harvest. It is also important to know how to store and preserve your crop – especially if you still have a glut despite your planning. This section provides invaluable tips and short- and long-term storage, including bottling, drying, freezing and pickling.

The vegetable gardener will always face a fight against invaders and attackers from the animal and plant world. But happily there are ways of dealing with these problems, even if gardening organically. From aphids to mildew, this section delineates the most common pests, diseases and weeds, explaining what they are, how to protect against them and how to treat them, including attracting beneficial wildlife and using natural pesticides.

The last section acts as a kind of directory that will take you through the specific crops, giving you tips for the best varieties, when to plant, how to grow, how to protect, when and how to harvest and how to prepare for eating. Divided into basic plant groups, it covers the Cabbage Family, Peas, Beans and Corn, Salad and Leafy Crops, the Gourd Family (such as cucumbers and squashes), the Onion Family, Soft Vegetables (such as tomatoes and peppers), Root Crops and Herbs.

Foreword

While buying local food is a first step to enjoying really fresh seasonal vegetables, there is nothing quite like having your pan of water simmering at the ready, popping out to your plot with a basket over your arm, plucking your baby carrots from the soil and eating them within 10 minutes! Scrummy!

It used to be considered quite a luxury to grow vegetables – processed food was all the rage, and cheap. It simply wasn't fashionable to want to grow your own, particularly when there were so many other demands on your time. Thankfully, all that has changed over the last few years. Yes, food prices have risen and, yes, we are told that 'staycations' are in vogue as we stay at home to save money, but the real change is that we have started to value our food much more highly.

We used to think 'reduced' was the best word to read on a label ('reduced sugar' or 'reduced fat'), then we moved on to 'added' ('added vitamins', 'added omega 3'). But now we have moved full circle and realize that by far the best option is real, unprocessed fresh food. As we value our food more, we accept that prices have to rise if fresh and tasty food is to be a priority. The knock-on effect is that growing your own vegetables has become really economical, as well as beneficial for the environment and our own wellbeing. As the saying goes, 'Gardening is a way of showing that you believe in tomorrow'.

This book successfully simplifies the whole process and encourages us to 'get on with it' and start growing in whatever space we have. The full explanation of 'where', 'what', 'why' and 'how' will help to get us on our way in minutes rather than weeks. Rachelle Strauss speaks from experience, having 'got on with it' herself, and in her down-to-earth style does not wash over the cost savings. We soon understand which crops will save most money and how to ensure we make the best of a glut of fruit or veg. (I know from my own experience one of the best savings that can be made is on the easiest to grow salad crops. This year I have saved at least £25 by growing my own salad leaves rather than buying bags in the supermarket.)

Growing your own food is extremely satisfying, children love getting involved, and it does really help the waistline in more ways than one! If you are thinking of growing a Carrot Crunch Lunch, then this is the book for you.

Happy Grow Your Own!

Heather Gorringe
CEO, Wiggly Wigglers

Introduction

An increasing number of people are doing their bit for the environment, staying healthy and saving money by using their gardens, windowsills and greenhouses to grow food. With high food prices and concerns about sustainable farming methods, there has never been a better time to get your hands in the soil and have a go at growing your own food. Indeed, with a waiting list of more than 40 years for allotments in some parts of the UK, growing your own vegetables has never been so popular.

Reduce the Cost of Your Food

Food prices have been increasing at three times the rate of inflation over the past few years. The effect has been a rise in the average family's shopping bill of £750 a year. Coupled with rising energy costs and increased mortgages, more households have found it a challenge to make ends meet. According to the United Nations Food and Agriculture Organization, global food prices will go on rising and could be 20 per cent higher in ten years' time. There is one satisfying way to make your household budget go further, however, and that's to grow some of your own food!

Reasons for Increased Food Prices

▶ Poor weather conditions leading to poor harvests.
▶ Global shortages in key crops.
▶ Increasing demand for Western food from developing countries such as China.

▶ The rising cost of oil leading to higher transportation costs.

▶ Land that was used to grow food is being used to grow biofuels.

Improve Your Health

There are numerous health benefits to be gained from growing your own food. Doing so will enable you to:

▶ Eat better quality food for less money.

▶ Decide what fertilizers and pesticides you are prepared to use and can grow organically if you wish.

▶ Get exercise in the fresh air as you potter around your vegetable plot.

▶ Reduce the amount of GM food you eat by growing your own.

▶ Be out in the sunshine, which can elevate mood and promote healthy bones.

▶ Keep your brain active: research shows gardening to be useful for people with signs of dementia.

▶ Reduce stress and tension.

▶ More easily eat the recommended 5-a-day portions of fruit and vegetables.

▶ Ditch the unhealthy snacks: home-grown food tastes fantastic, so you'll be more inclined to eat it than indulge in 'fast foods'.

▶ Get maximum nutrition from your food because you can eat seasonally and harvest and eat it straight away.

▶ Enjoy a diet that is high in fibre and low in calories.

▶ Reduce the risk of high blood pressure, strokes, certain cancers, cataracts, birth defects and diabetes.

Help the Environment

Growing your own vegetables gives you the opportunity to lower your carbon footprint. Not only will you save on food miles (the miles from farm to your plate), but you'll also reduce the number of miles you have to travel to buy your food. Instead of driving to an out-of-town supermarket, you'll be able to step into your garden or walk to your allotment for your food.

Making Environmental Choices

Will you grow organically, biodynamically or carefully choose the chemical fertilizers and pest controls that you will allow on to the food you eat? You can reduce the number of chemical pesticides that modern, intensive farming relies on and this will have a knock-on effect on the environment. If you choose to grow organically, you'll find your garden will become a haven for bees and butterflies, you'll benefit your local environment by not polluting rivers, the earth or the air, and you'll help local wildlife to thrive.

Who Can Garden?

Gardening is the perfect activity for everyone, whatever age and fitness level. Gardening can be as gentle or strenuous as you like – you can always get somebody else to help you with the really tough parts like digging! Once you have your garden set up, it can take just an hour or so a week to maintain, depending on size and conditions. But if you wish, it can become a full-time hobby or lifestyle commitment.

Getting Children Involved

Gardening can be a richly rewarding experience for children, an education for life. A study conducted by the Early Learning Centre showed that 86 per cent of under-sixes watched up to six hours of TV a day. Imagine if some of that time was spent gardening instead!

Encouraging Healthy Activity

Bupa says that around 15 per cent of children in the UK are obese, and recommends that all children should be doing at least 60 minutes of physical activity each day to prevent serious health problems. It advises that physically inactive pastimes, such as watching television or playing computer games, should be limited to less than two hours a day.

Encouraging Exploration

Most children love the opportunity to get their hands muddy, explore creepy crawlies and grow their own food. Give them a small plot or container, something that they know is theirs to take care of, but isn't overwhelming, and help them to choose easy-to-grow food.

Gardening and the Elderly

Gardening is a great activity for elderly people too. It can be done at a gentle pace and, as long as you do a few stretches to warm up before you start, you'll benefit from the walking, bending, stretching and lifting that is required to maintain your garden.

Making Adjustments

If you're unable to stretch or lift well, there are lightweight, long-handled tools available, as well as special stools to help you kneel down. Alternatively, grow vegetables in pots or in raised beds to reduce the amount of bending down you need to do. If you have poor eyesight, arthritis or need to use a wheelchair, your garden can be adapted and designed to work for you, so that you can still enjoy the benefits of growing your own food.

Gardening is Easy!

If you think gardening is for people with unlimited time, space, energy and money then think again! Gardening can be as easy or challenging as you wish. The aim of this book is to show you how easy it is to start with even a tiny plot, minimal time and little money. By the time you have finished this book, you'll feel confident to take the first steps and have a go at growing some of your own food.

Container Gardening

An entire allotment would require at least a few hours a week of your time, but maintaining one raised bed might take only a few minutes a week. If you have less time and space available, why not think about growing vegetables in a window box or hanging basket, which you can take care of in just a few minutes a day? An assortment of containers on a patio will provide you with a variety of food for minimum input.

About This Book

Throughout the chapters of this book you will learn:

▶ How to get the most from your soil and lightconditions.

▶ Whether you should use a polytunnel or greenhouse.

▶ How to design your perfect garden layout.

▶ How to choose the best vegetables to grow.

▶ All about preparing the ground.

▶ How to choose the right compost, fertilizer and tools.

▶ When and how to sow.

▶ All about harvesting and preserving your food.

▶ How to deal with pests and weeds.

▶ How to grow more than 40 varieties of vegetables and herbs.

▶ The easiest crops to grow if you are a beginner.

▶ How to grow food without a garden.

Why Grow Your Own?

Saving Money

There are many benefits to growing your own vegetables, including environmental or health-based ones, but one big one is that it's cheaper. You can save a lot of money by doing a little 'Digging for Victory'!

Cost-saving Crops

There are great financial savings to be made on many crops, especially new potatoes, spinach, cherry tomatoes and runner beans, all of which are easy to grow.

Some Sample Crops

New potatoes cost around £1.25 per kilogram to buy, depending on type. Buying five seed potatoes costs about £1.50 and you can harvest anything from 350 g (12 oz) to over 850 g (30 oz) per seed potato. Allowing for an average yield, this works out at 60p per kilo for delicious new potatoes! A 2.5 kg (5 1/2 lb) net of seed potatoes contains approximately 25–30 tubers and costs approximately £4. If you were to get 500 g (18 oz) from each potato, you'd be harvesting 14 kg (31 lb) of new potatoes for around 29p a kilogram!

Little Gem lettuces are another great cost-saver. A packet containing 120 seeds costs about £1.50. This means for £1.50 you and your family could potentially grow, harvest and eat 120 lettuces. If you bought 120 Little Gem lettuces from the supermarket, you would have to spend more than £45!

Top Tip
One of the best places to store unused vegetable seeds is your fridge.

A Frugal Hobby

If you think gardening is a hobby for the well off, then think again. There are many ways to make gardening a frugal experience. And once you get proficient at growing your own vegetables, you can save even more money by saving your own seeds and using them the following year.

Sharing Seeds and Crops

You can swap seeds, seedlings, mature plants and harvested crops with friends, family, work colleagues and neighbours. Most people end up with too many of one type of seed or plant, so why not split the cost with someone else by planning your gardens together? You could grow tomatoes, basil and runner beans, while your friend grows beetroot, dwarf beans and potatoes, for example.

Freecycling and Borrowing

Don't rush out and buy lots of new tools straight away: ask around and see what you can borrow, share or get for free. Freecycle is a great place to get pots, forks and spades for nothing. Your neighbour might have hung up his secateurs long ago and be happy to give you a long-term loan. Put up an advertisement in a local shop; in exchange for a loan, perhaps you could offer some of your harvest.

Selling Your Harvest

If you discover you are more green-fingered than you thought, you could sell excess plants or crops at a local table sale. Your profit could be put towards next year's seeds or new tools. You might even decide to preserve some of your crops and sell them, for example as chutneys and pickles. Or you could sell carrot cakes at a local car boot sale.

Protecting the Environment

With signs of global warming on the increase, many people are looking to make lifestyle changes that benefit the environment. The way we obtain our food is unrecognizable from 50 years ago. We buy the same food all year round instead of shopping seasonally; we buy more processed and 'convenience' food than ever before; we like to pay as little for our food as possible, and we no longer shop locally. Choosing food that is local and seasonal means it does not have to travel so far. Reducing food miles can have a dramatic effect on reducing carbon dioxide emissions.

Did You Know?

Air freight emits more greenhouse gases per food mile than any other mode of transport.

Food Miles

'Food miles' means the distance food travels from the farm to your plate. It is estimated that one third of your household's impact on climate change comes from the food you choose to eat, including the country your food originates from, where you purchase it, how you get to the shop, how you store your food and how much food waste you create.

In the UK, food travels 30 billion kilometres (18.6 billion miles) each year and is responsible for the UK emitting nearly 19 million tonnes of carbon dioxide into the atmosphere each year. By growing your own vegetables you'll be able to cut your personal carbon footprint and reduce the amount of CO2 you are responsible for emitting.

Seasonal Eating

Let's face it, most of us are creatures of habit when it comes to our meals. Many of us buy the same foods week in, week out, enjoying out-of-season produce. We want to eat apples in spring, swede in summer, salad in autumn and tomatoes in winter. Subsequently, more than half the vegetables eaten in the UK are imported. We love our exotic foods too. Instead of eating traditional British food, grown in season, we enjoy a variety of foods from all over the world such as mangoes, spices, cocoa and rice. By growing your own vegetables you'll be able to enjoy seasonal produce and learn new ways of eating your favourite foods.

The High Cost of Exotic Food

According to DEFRA, food transport accounts for 25 per cent of all HGV vehicle kilometres in the UK (source https://statistics.defra.gov.uk/esg/reports/foodmiles/execsumm.pdf). In addition, transport of food by air has the highest CO2 emissions per tonne and it's having a massive environmental impact. Air transportation generates 177 times more greenhouse gases than shipping and is growing at a rate of six per cent per year because it is quicker and more convenient than shipping.

Processed Food

Convenience meals and processed food travel miles to reach you! A pizza will be made up from different components from different countries, for example:

- ▶ Flour: 5,400 miles from North America
- ▶ Tomatoes: 1,000 miles from Italy
- ▶ Tuna: 5,600 miles from Mauritius

- **Pineapple:** 4,500 miles from Kenya
- **Peppers:** 400 miles from Holland
- **Black pepper:** 5,000 miles from India
- **Mozzarella cheese:** 1,000 miles from Italy

In addition, each individual ingredient, once it reaches the country, travels from factory to factory before making its way as a finished pizza to the shop. By the time your 'convenient' pizza reaches you, it will have accumulated more than 20,000 food miles!

Make Your Own

By growing your own vegetables, you'll be able to make more of your meals from scratch. You'll be able to make your own 'convenience' foods, such as soups, stews and pasta sauces from the ingredients you grow. This is healthier for you and will help reduce food miles further.

The High Cost of 'Cheap' Food

Our desire for 'cheap' food is also responsible for increased food miles. Many foods, such as fish, are sent abroad, where labour costs are much cheaper, to be processed, before being sent back to the UK to be sold. We've turned food into a quick, cheap and convenient product to refuel our bodies.

Did you know?

The amount of food air freighted around the world has risen by 140 per cent since 1992.

The cost to the farming industry is massive. Many small, family-run farms using traditional methods of growing cannot compete with large-scale, industrialized agricultural corporations. Larger conglomerates can sell far more cheaply to supermarkets, but by doing so they undercut individual farmers. The real cost of cheap food is not always noticed, but thanks to prominent campaigners, such as Hugh Fearnley-Whittingstall, more people are becoming aware of the effects our demand for cheap food is having on our health, farming industry and environment.

Reduce Personal Travel

We travel further for our shopping than ever before and often use a car to get there. Whereas we once walked to our local grocer, baker and butcher – perhaps two or three times a week – we'll now get in the car and drive to a large, out-of-town supermarket for a once-weekly stock up. More than two million tonnes of carbon dioxide is produced in the UK by cars travelling to and from shops.

'Local' Produce

Once you get to the supermarket, you may see advertisements for 'local produce', but because they are part of a huge supermarket chain, you might find that your 'local' potatoes have in fact travelled by lorry to a central distribution depot to be sorted and packed before being taken back to your nearest store!

Did you know?

The Soil Association has decided that in order to qualify as 'organic', all air-freighted food will have to meet ethical trade standards from 2009.

When you add together all of these factors, it is estimated that the average food has travelled 1,500 miles before it gets on to your plate. You can reduce that figure dramatically by growing some of your own produce. You won't need to get the car out to go and collect fresh vegetables from your garden!

Beware the Lure of the Supermarket

How many times have you popped into the supermarket to buy a couple of potatoes and found those potatoes cost you £20? By the time you've succumbed to the '3-for-2' bargain, scanned the 'reduced' items, bought a couple of 'must-have' items, stocked up your cupboard with the kids' favourite cereal and treated yourself to a chocolate bar, you're eating very expensive potatoes. In addition, you might have clocked up some wear and tear on your car, been frustrated about the person who grabbed your parking space, had to queue for ages and been diverted on the way home due to road works. Now imagine opening your back door, stepping outside on a perfect summer evening, taking your fork and digging up your own potatoes. You've saved yourself all that time, reduced your carbon footprint and replaced stress with enormous satisfaction!

> ## Did you know?
> Cars are responsible for 20 per cent of the UK's CO_2 emissions from food transport.

Protect the Land

Our land is being eroded and contaminated by harsh farming methods. Our natural environment is being polluted with modern chemicals. We are losing top soil faster than it can be replenished and our reliance on chemicals is increasing.

High cost of land and labour in the UK means we import more, which means we, as a nation, are becoming more and more dependent on the rest of the world for our food. Not very empowering or 'self-sufficient', is it?

However, when you consider that the majority of the money you spend on food has gone into processing, packaging, transportation, storage and advertising, you'll begin to understand that 'value' and 'cost' are not the same thing. We're paying more to the marketing and packaging companies than the farmers who produce our food!

Reduce Chemicals

In order to keep up with growing demand for cheap food, farmers resort to getting as much out of the soil as they can for one harvest. They are unable to afford the luxury of leaving land fallow to restore itself the natural way, so use chemicals to replenish the soil with the minimum required nutrients. This means that foods are losing their nutritional value. According to Elmer Heinrich, author of The Root of All Disease, you'd have to eat 10 servings of spinach to get the same level of minerals from just one serving about 50 years ago. Over-farming depletes nutrients from the soil, which means they are not there for the plants to absorb; this is particularly true of trace minerals, which are essential for good health.

Nutritious Vegetables from Nutrient-rich Soil

Vegetables are no longer grown for their high nutritional content, but for their uniform size, disease and pest resistance and longevity once picked. A tomato is the perfect example. Once you have tasted a home-grown tomato, picked fresh from the vine on a warm summer's day, you'll realize that what you have been buying from supermarkets all these years is, in comparison, tasteless mush designed to look right on the shelf. The USDA has compared nutrient loss in 1975 with that in 2001 and found, for example:

- ▶ **Broccoli:** Calcium and vitamin C content are down 50 per cent.

- ▶ **Cauliflower:** Vitamin C down 45 per cent, vitamin B1 down 48 per cent and vitamin B2 down 47 per cent.

By growing your own vegetables, you can improve the nutritional quality of the food you eat. You won't need to employ intensive farming methods, you can feed the soil and

choose varieties based on their nutritional content and taste rather than superficial qualities such as shape and size.

Attract Wildlife

By dedicating some of your space to growing vegetables, you'll benefit the environment enormously and attract bees, butterflies, birds and insects to your garden. They, in turn, will pollinate your crops. It's the perfect harmonious relationship!

Did You Know?

Bees are responsible for pollinating one third of the food you eat. Imagine a life without bees…

Grow Organically

By growing organically, you'll be doing even more to improve the environment. You won't be buying crops that have been sprayed with polluting ingredients, you won't be contaminating the air, earth and water, you won't be killing pests or weeds with toxic chemicals, which in turn upsets the delicate balance of the ecosystem. Rather, you will be taking care of your soil and local environment and be doing your bit to slow down climate change.

Reduce Waste

According to WRAP, the average household in the UK throws away one third of the food it buys, which amounts to 6.7 million tonnes of food each year. Of that waste, 40 per cent by weight of the food thrown away that could have been eaten is made up of fresh fruit and vegetables. If you grow your own vegetables, you'll be able to pick exactly the amount you need when you need it. This will dramatically decrease your food waste.

The Main Causes of Food Waste

▶ Cooking too much and throwing away the extras.
▶ Changing plans (eating a takeaway instead of cooking at home).
▶ Buying 3-for-2 offers and not using things before they go off.
▶ Impulse buys.
▶ Poor portion control.
▶ Incorrect storage.

Did You Know?

The UK imports about 350,000 tonnes of potatoes per year, many of which have been in storage for up to six months.

Landfills and Greenhouse Gas Emissions

Many people think that throwing food in the landfill is OK: it's biodegradable, so doesn't create problems. The trouble is, more often than not, the biodegradable food gets wrapped inside a non-biodegradable plastic bag! If the air cannot get to the food then it won't rot down. In the absence of oxygen, biodegradable materials such as food, cardboard and green waste decompose and produce methane gas. Methane contributes 23 times more to climate change than the equivalent amount of CO_2. If we ended food waste, we would reduce greenhouse gas emissions to the equivalent of taking one in five cars off the road.

Food Packaging

In addition to the food itself, around 6.3 million tonnes of packaging comes into our homes every year. Around one sixth of your food budget goes on packaging and makes up a third of our household waste. How many of us have struggled to get into a shrink-wrapped swede, found a sweating potato in the corner of our pre-packed purchase or bought tomatoes on a polystyrene tray? It's crazy when you think that after all your effort it ends up in the bin anyway!

Reducing Packaging Waste

Although packaging is required in some instances to reduce food waste, not all of it is necessary. Many vegetables, for example onions, come in their own packaging. Cabbages don't need plastic shrink-wrap; most people pull off the outer leaves anyway. It's better to select your own potatoes, rather than buy the pre-weighed, pre-packaged bags. Unfortunately, a lot of food is packaged in plastic, and recycling facilities are limited. Most of our plastic waste ends up in the landfill, where it sits around for the next few hundred years.

The 3 Rs

Gardening is a great excuse to get creative with reusing and recycling to reduce your household landfill waste. Here are 13 ideas:

▶ **Seeding pots:** Reuse old food containers, such as yogurt pots, soft cheese containers or juice cartons.

▶ **Biodegradable pots:** Make biodegradable seedling pots from toilet roll inners or old newspapers.

▶ **A new way for potatoes:** Grow potatoes in a stack of tyres.

▶ **Creative plant pots:** Old saucepans, rusty cake tins, holey buckets, even old shoes make original and useful plant pots.

▶ **Drainage materials:** Use broken crocs and polystyrene.

▶ **Plant ties:** A great use for old socks and tights, wire coat hangers, strips of cloth and those annoying plastic ties that attach toys to their packaging.

▶ **Mini cloche:** Simply cut a two-litre plastic bottle in half.

▶ **Mini propagators:** Try using the hard plastic containers that cherry tomatoes or soft fruits (or some indulgent cakes!) come in.

▶ **Seed containers:** Empty spice pots or baby food jars are ideal.

▶ **Plant markers:** Cut strips from margarine containers, yogurt pots or even old Venetian blinds.

▶ **Bird scarers:** Thread and hang old CDs to keep birds away from your crops.

▶ **Recycle net bags:** Onions, oranges and other produce sometimes come in small net bags that can be reused to keep cabbage white butterflies off your crops or for air-drying shallots and onions.

▶ **Make your own compost:** Turn all fruit and vegetable peelings into food for your soil.

Capture Rainwater

Don't forget to capture the greatest gift of all – rainwater! Set up a few water butts and you'll be able to reduce your water footprint too. If you're on a water meter you'll see instant savings.

Health

If you grow your own vegetables, you'll be able to eat well for minimal cost. You'll also be able to preserve vegetables within minutes of picking to retain as much nutrition as possible. There are many other therapeutic benefits to be gained from gardening, including physical wellbeing, improved cognitive function and social satisfaction. Growing your own can have knock-on effects on your state of mind, as you'll discover later, which can keep tension and stress at bay.

Top Tip

Store vegetables uncut until you want to use them to prevent loss of valuable nutrients.

A Healthy Diet

Growing your own vegetables means you know exactly what you are eating. You don't have to worry about pesticide residue, the freshness of your food, GM crops or how long a product has been stored before you eat it. You'll be in full control of the food you and your family eat and your health may improve as a result.

Fresh Food is Nutritious Food

Eating fresh food means you eat more nutritionally rich foods, so you might not need to eat 10 times the amount of spinach after all! Vitamin C can be lost quickly in many foods, especially green leafy vegetables. If you can pick them fresh and prepare them within minutes, the vitamin and mineral content will be much higher.

Did You Know?

In 2007, Newcastle University found that organic tomatoes, potatoes, cabbage, onions and lettuce had between 20 and 40 per cent more nutrients than non-organic produce.

Trimming, dicing and slicing also results in leaching of vitamins B, C and E. Many supermarket prepared vegetables are washed and trimmed before being packaged. If you dig up a carrot, bring it in to prepare and cook it for your next meal, you'll be getting more nutrition on your plate!

Avoiding Nutrition Loss

A vegetable's skin, rinds and peelings protect the vegetables and keep vitamins locked in. However, our obsession with convenience foods means we regularly buy produce with the tops and tails trimmed, such as radishes or dwarf beans; or with a thin outer layer removed, such as scraped fluorescent orange carrots and brilliant white parsnips. Once this has happened, the product begins to degrade and lose vitamin C. If you regularly buy imported produce, then the nutrient loss might be even greater.

Consider the difference between a washed and trimmed dwarf bean flown in from Kenya compared to stepping out on to your patio, picking your own and taking it straight to the kitchen to prepare. You can be pretty sure that growing your own vegetables organically, and harvesting and preparing your food close to eating can benefit your health in a myriad of ways.

Eat Well for Less

People tend to give up 'luxury' food and look for cheaper options such as value lines or convenience foods when money is sparse. However, when people are stressed about the state of their finances, they sometimes turn to

comfort food. According to German scientists, there is a significant link between being in debt and obesity. A study of more than 9,000 individuals found that a quarter of those who were seriously in debt were clinically obese. The researchers blame the trend on the high price of healthy food and a tendency for people worried by debt to 'comfort eat'. Unfortunately, foods such as sweets or fatty snacks are usually less expensive than fruit or vegetables.

Gardening and Physical Wellbeing

When money is tight, luxury items and leisure activities are the first things we give up. With the credit crunch on us, people are cancelling gym memberships in favour of exercising at home, or worse, giving up exercise altogether. Gyms all over the country are offering reduced rates and special offers to try to get people back in through their doors. However, you can save yourself money and get your exercise by growing your own vegetables.

Gardening as Exercise

Gardening can be as relaxed or strenuous as you like. More strenuous tasks include digging over new ground and digging trenches for potatoes, which will tone your muscles and increase your heart rate. Weeding involves lots of bending, stretching and squatting to keep you supple. Meanwhile, a gentle stroll around your plot every day gets you out into the fresh air in all weathers and improves the circulation.

Some of the Benefits of a Gardening Work-out

▶ **Take the pressure off:** Thirty minutes of gardening each day can help lower blood pressure and cholesterol levels.

▶ **Prevention better than cure:** Gardening has been found to help prevent heart disease, strokes and type II diabetes.

▶ **The sunshine vitamin:** Sunlight helps the body make vitamin D, which is essential for healthy bones.

▶ **A weapon against illness:** Gardening can help slow down the degenerative process of some illnesses.

▶ **Do it your way:** You can work at your own pace and you don't need to be clad in Lycra or the latest trainers to reap the benefits. There is no need to feel self-conscious, like you might at the gym – no one is watching or comparing you!

Did You Know?

It is estimated that you can burn around 272 calories per hour by gardening!

Gardening and Mental Health

For those with mental illness or depression, gardening can bring a great sense of achievement and reward. It also gives a sense of hope: planting a seed, knowing that with time, care and the correct attention it will provide you with food is

33

incredibly satisfying and gives a sense of purpose, increased self-confidence and inspiration. The results of gardening on physical and mental health have been so profound that some hospitals and prisons have gardens for patients and inmates to take care of. Many studies have shown that gardening can help beat depression and relieve stress.

Did You Know?

A survey carried out by MIND found 50 per cent of people believed that physical exercise, including gardening, was one of the best activities to boost their mental health.

Gardening and General Wellbeing

In addition to its many proven physical benefits and mental health benefits as above, gardening can improve your emotional and mental wellbeing in the following ways:

▶ **The path to calm:** The peace and tranquillity of gardening can help remove tension and lower stress levels.

▶ **A natural drug:** A particular type of bacteria, Mycobacterium vaccae, that is found in soil is said to function like an antidepressant.

▶ **An aid to recovery:** Gardening can help you recover after illness or a difficult time in your life.

▶ **The confidence of learning:** You can learn new skills and who knows where they might take you?

Children and Gardening

Children are more likely to eat something they have grown themselves and it's easier to ensure they eat their recommended five-a-day portions of fruit and vegetables if you grow some of your own.

Encouraging New Experiences

If your children don't like tomatoes, a tiny cherry tomato picked straight from the vine might be what they need to change their minds. If they don't like spinach, then grow rainbow chard instead. If they have been involved with the sowing, growing and harvesting then the chances are they will experiment more with their food.

Top Tip

Give your child a sense of ownership by allocating them their 'own' patch to cultivate.

Produce picked straight from the garden is usually more tender than shop bought because it is fresher. Courgettes are creamy rather than bitter, broad beans melt in your mouth, runner beans don't have tough strings that need removing and cabbages actually have taste!

Educational Benefits

Knowledge is power: showing a child where food comes from and how it is grown fosters an interest that will give them the confidence to try new things. A UK survey showed that a third of UK children were unable to identify celery, more than 20 per cent did not recognize a potato and 5.5 per cent could not name a carrot. You can put your child top of the class just by gardening with them!

36

The Good Life

We are working longer hours than ever before, but more people are realizing that working long hours and earning money isn't the lifestyle they want. There is a growing trend towards a simpler life and self-sufficiency. What better way to start than by growing some of your own food?

Did You Know?

You think you don't have time to look after a garden? The average person spends 3.8 hours a day watching television!

Creative Downsizing

Some families find that if one partner can grow food and cook healthy meals from scratch, they save more money than they would if that person went out to work. By the time you've both come home late from a stressful day at work, eaten a takeaway, gone on expensive holidays because you're overworked, treated the kids because you feel guilty for not spending more time together and bought new clothes and gadgets to make yourself feel better, you've spent more than the money you've earned! By spending a couple of hours a week growing your own food, it will give you a taste of the good life and provide you with experiences to make informed decisions. From there, you can decide if downshifting even more would suit your lifestyle.

The Importance of Quality Time

A knock-on effect of working long hours, juggling extra-curricular activities and attending various clubs is that we spend less quality time with the people we love. More often than not, we come home exhausted in the evenings and, while the kids might go off to their computers or out with their friends, we sit in silence being hypnotized by the box in the corner of the room.

Gardening Teamwork

Gardening together allows you to spend quality time working as a family towards a common goal. You can forget about your stresses, put your grievances to one side and work as a team at something that is meaningful and has great rewards. And how satisfying it is to sit down to a meal together that you have grown in your own garden!

Creating Community

Gardening can be as solitary or social an activity as you wish. What better way to break the ice with new neighbours than to offer them some home-grown produce? If you take on an allotment, you'll never be short of people to ask for

advice, swap tips or share stories with. If you take part in a community gardening project you'll make new friends in no time.

Better-tasting Food

If you're fed up with watery potatoes and tasteless mushy tomatoes, don't put up with second-rate vegetables a moment longer! Gardening puts you back in control of the food you eat.

Cultivating Heirloom Varieties

You can also do your part for future generations by growing varieties that we are in danger of losing for ever. You can be a part of history by keeping the heritage of growing our own food alive! You might be able to find native species to your area or find some old varieties that are rarely seen in the shops any more. You can swap your tasteless shop-bought produce for food that is bursting with flavour and nutrition.

Self-sufficiency

And finally, what more satisfying reason for growing your own than being independent? Instead of relying on shops to provide all your food, you can grow some of your own. It's a great way to get a taste of 'the good life'! You don't need a mansion with an estate to grow your own food: as you'll be shown in later chapters, even a window box can provide you with enough salad for the summer. You can start right now with a few containers and a willingness to learn.

Checklist

▶ How much **money** could you save by growing just one type of vegetable?

▶ Are there people you could **share tools or swap seeds** with?

▶ How many of the vegetables you eat are **imported**? Do you eat **seasonally** or are you a creature of habit?

▶ How much **processed or convenience food** do you buy each week? Is there one meal you could create from some home-grown vegetables?

▶ How many **miles** do you travel each week to buy food? How much could you reduce that by growing some of your own food instead?

▶ How many times have you been into the supermarket to top up on vegetables and ended up buying other i**tems you never intended to buy**?

▶ How much of the food you eat is **organic**?

▶ How much **food waste** does your household create? (Try actually weighing it for a reality check!)

▶ How much **food packaging** do you put into the landfill waste every week?

▶ Take a look through your household rubbish. Which items could you **reuse** for gardening?

▶ How many '**prepared' vegetables** do you buy?

▶ Are you spending enough time outdoors? Could gardening be a way for you to enjoy spending **quality time** with your family and friends?

Where To Grow

Making the Most of Your Space

You don't need a huge garden or allotment to grow your own vegetables. You can get started right now with whatever space you have. You can even garden without a garden! If you live in a flat, you can grow food on your windowsills, in a window box or on a balcony. If you have a tiny garden, you can grow vegetables in containers, hanging baskets and grow bags. If your garden is larger, you can use borders, beds or raised beds to grow food. If you have no space at all, or want more, think about renting an allotment, joining a community garden or getting involved with a landshare scheme.

Thinking Laterally… and Vertically

Whatever space you have, you don't need to be limited by it when you grow your own food. With careful planning, you can get the best out of your space and get a taste for self-sufficiency. There are 'mini' varieties of vegetables to try and most herbs are best contained in pots anyway. If space is limited, think about growing upwards or downwards rather than sideways. For example, you could grow tumbling tomatoes and runner beans rather than crops that take up a lot of room. Don't forget to make the most of your windowsills too.

Did You Know?

Fifty thousand tonnes of salad products are thrown away by UK households every year, costing consumers over £150 million.

Growing Vegetables in Containers

If you have a patio or balcony, you can use containers for growing vegetables. Container gardening can be very successful as long as you add drainage holes at the bottom of each pot and are prepared to spend more time watering your plants. There are some great books to help you select the right varieties for whatever sized pot you have. Everything from beans to tomatoes can be grown in the right sized container. If you have no outdoor space at all, you can try hanging baskets, window boxes and windowsills.

Top Tip

Growing herbs in pots will prevent them taking over your garden and provide tastier, more tender results.

Hanging Baskets

Heavy crops, such as pumpkins, are unsuitable for hanging baskets, but most compact or sprawling plants are worth a go, and hanging baskets are perfect for herbs because they drain well. Tumbling varieties of tomatoes are perfect for hanging baskets. Remember to turn the hanging basket so that all the tomatoes get some sunlight. Peas, which normally require staking, can be planted in a hanging basket and left to scramble over the sides.

Make sure the basket is on a strong bracket, as they can get quite heavy, and water your plants once or twice a day, even if it rains. Position the hanging basket so that you can reach it easily.

Window Boxes and Windowsills

In a window box, you can grow a variety of salad leaves and herbs. Cut-and-come-again salad leaves are the ideal crop for beginners. You're not limited to lettuce either – rocket, baby spinach, mizuna and mustard leaf will give you a 'posh salad' any day of the week, or how about spring onions garnished with basil, parsley and chives?

Top Tip

The corner of a conservatory is the ideal place to grow sun-loving herbs and vegetables such as tomatoes and basil.

Most people have at least one sunny windowsill in their home. Think of it as a mini greenhouse! You can grow sun-loving herbs such as rosemary or basil, compact tomatoes, chillies, aubergines and even rocket. Just make sure the plants don't get scorched on a really hot day and turn the plants so that each side gets some sun.

Borders and Beds

If you have a larger garden, you can use traditional borders and beds for growing vegetables. You might like straight rows of delicious crops ready to be picked, but you don't have to plant in uniform rows. You might prefer to grow them in between your favourite flowers, or it might be more practical to make a couple of raised beds for ease of use. Whatever your preference, you can design your perfect garden.

Light

Light is essential for plants. Before choosing which vegetables and herbs you are going to grow, you need to check their light requirements and compare it to your chosen plot. Some plants can tolerate more shade than others.

Aspect

If you are going to grow crops on a windowsill or in a window box, make a note of which direction your windows face and which ones get the most sunlight at different times of the day. If you are planning to grow vegetables on a patio or balcony, check for shadows cast from buildings, trees or other immovable objects and see how much sunlight this area gets. You'll need to spend some time watching the sun move around your garden and arrange to grow your food in the sunniest site.

Choosing the Best Site

A south-facing aspect is best for growing vegetables and herbs. You might have a south-facing wall or window box or even be lucky enough to have a south-facing garden. East- or west-facing areas usually get full sunlight for half of the day or dappled sunlight all day long. North-facing gardens are more challenging for successful planting as they don't get much sun at all. To get a real idea of the light conditions of your garden, draw a rough sketch of it and dedicate a sunny day to jot down hourly details of which parts of your garden get sun and which parts are in the shade. By the end of the day you will have an objective plan showing the sunlight conditions of your garden.

Did you know?

Most vegetable plants need six to eight hours per day of sunlight to grow properly.

Growing in a Shady Spot

Although some vegetables, such as tomatoes or peppers, will not grow at all without full sunlight, others will grow in partial shade, so don't worry if you're not getting full sunlight on your chosen plot. Some plants prefer less light and cooler conditions and will do well with less than six hours of sun. You'll need to ensure you leave extra spacing between crops to compensate for the lack of light, but it's worth

experimenting to find out which crops you can grow despite less-than-optimum light conditions. By careful use of pots and baskets, however, you can turn things to get more sun. If all else fails, you could start a mushroom farm!

Shade-tolerant Crops

Crops that will tolerate less sun include root vegetables such as beetroot and radishes. Herbs that will tolerate shadier conditions include mint, parsley, fennel, chives and coriander. Salad leaves, including lettuces and spinach, don't like it too hot otherwise they can bolt easily. Broccoli and kale will grow well in a more shaded plot.

Top Tip

Plant crops in height order to prevent shading.

Greenhouses and Polytunnels

If you have room for a greenhouse or polytunnel, you can extend your growing season. Both provide a light, warm place to start off seedlings and allow you to grow crops into the autumn. Tomatoes are a prime example of a crop that grows well in a greenhouse (although you don't need a greenhouse to grow them) and salad leaves will enjoy the protection of a polytunnel well into the autumn months.

Polytunnel Pros and Cons

A polytunnel is a metal frame covered with a semi-circular Polythene tunnel. Polytunnels stay very warm and, due to their higher temperatures than outside, it is possible to grow more exotic vegetables and herbs, plus you can enjoy a longer harvesting season.

Polytunnel Pros

▶ Much warmer than greenhouses, and they don't scorch plants in the summer like greenhouses can
▶ Cheaper than greenhouses
▶ Easier to move

Polytunnel Cons

▶ Less stable – need to be situated in a sheltered spot or a high wind can take the entire construction down
▶ More difficult to ventilate than greenhouses – can become very humid
▶ They can tear easily

49

Greenhouses

Greenhouses are constructed from thin glass and are useful for starting off seeds, protecting delicate seedlings and providing a sheltered place to take plants into during bad weather. Greenhouses can get extremely hot, so are ideal for growing crops like chillies, peppers and aubergines, but you must ventilate them well. During the winter, greenhouses can be heated, although this is not particularly environmentally friendly. Greenhouses vary a lot in price, depending on construction materials and build quality.

Disadvantages with Greenhouses

▶ A good greenhouse can be expensive

▶ Cheaper greenhouses warm up and cool down very quickly

▶ The glass in most greenhouses is very thin, so not suitable for use around young children

▶ Once it is up, a greenhouse is difficult to move

Top Tip

Keep greenhouses cooler by using sun shades during the hottest part of the day. This will prevent leaves getting scorched.

Soil Conditions

Having decided where to grow, it's time to get to know your soil. No two gardens are the same, and your soil might be slightly different to that in your neighbour's garden. Different plants have different requirements, so it's essential to know what type of soil you have.

Soil Types

Soil is made up of solids, liquids and air. The proportions of these determine which type of soil you have. You might have heard the terms chalky, clay, loam, peat, sandy or silty. These names basically describe the texture and main components of your soil. Knowing what type of soil you have can help you to get the most out of your gardening experience. Think of soil like car fuel; if your car runs on diesel, you won't get very far if you put petrol in the tank. Likewise, if you want to grow carrots, which prefer a free-draining sandy soil, you won't get much of a crop on a waterlogged clay soil.

Top Tip

Write a list of the vegetables you would like to grow and check to see what sort of soil type they prefer.

Chalky (or Limestone) Soil

Chalky soils are usually nutrient deficient and need yearly feeding with organic matter to make them more fertile. Chalky soils are very alkaline, so acid-loving plants don't thrive. Chalky soil is good for growing brassicas because the clubroot disease, which can affect this type of plant, is not usually an issue with this type of soil.

Pros

▶ Drains well
▶ Great for alkaline-loving plants
▶ Little risk of vegetables succumbing to clubroot disease

Cons

▶ Not very fertile
▶ No good for acid-loving crops

Clay Soil

Clay soil is made up of small particles that clump together. This means there are few air spaces between the particles, so nutrients and water are held in the soil. Pick up a small handful of soil and roll it between your fingers. Does it clump together straight away and form a sticky ball? If so, you probably have clay soil.

Pros

▶ Retains moisture so requires less water during the summer
▶ Holds nutrients well, so needs less fertilizer
▶ Generally very fertile

Cons

▶ Gets waterlogged easily and warms up later in the season

▶ Can bake like concrete in the summer, which can prevent plant roots reaching down or seedling heads pushing up

▶ Can be heavy to dig and very difficult to get to a friable texture without a lot of effort

Top Tip

Start a compost heap straight away! Most soils can be improved with lots of good quality compost.

Loamy Soil

Loamy soil has a good balance of particle sizes made up of clay, sand and silt. This makes it very easy to work with and means it holds water and nutrients at just the right level! Pick up a small handful of soil and roll it between your fingers. Does it feel soft and silky and roll into a soft ball? If so, you probably have loamy soil. Unfortunately, the only disadvantage is that it's quite hard to come by!

Pros

▶ Has a good balance of particle size

▶ Drains well so can be worked on all through the year

▶ Retains nutrients and contains lots of organic matter

Peat Soil

Peat soil is sometimes found in low-lying areas, though rarely in gardens. You might recognize it as an ingredient in bags of compost you have bought. Peat soil is very dark, rich and made up of organic matter. It retains moisture well and, as long as it has adequate drainage, it's a great growing medium. It does not usually need additional feeding but it is acidic, so unless you add lots of lime, you'll be unlikely to grow alkaline-loving crops.

Top Tip

Take soil samples from different parts of your garden and compare the results.

Pros

▶ Full of organic matter, so does not need extra feeding

▶ Moisture retentive, needing less water

▶ Great for acid-loving plants

Cons

▶ Can waterlog, so needs good drainage

▶ Can be too acidic for some plants

Sandy Soil

Sandy soil is made up of large particles that don't fuse together well. This means there are lots of air spaces between the particles and water and nutrients drain away quickly. Pick up a small handful of soil and roll it between your fingers. Does it feel gritty and not want to form a ball? If so, you probably have sandy soil.

Pros

▶ Drains very quickly so you can work on it during wetter months

▶ Warms quickly in the spring giving you a head start with planting

▶ Land easy to dig

▶ Root crops do well, especially carrots

Cons

▶ Needs watering more frequently, especially during the summer

▶ Loses nutrients quickly, so you need to add them with quality soil enhancers

▶ More likely to be eroded by wind or water

Silty Soil

Silty soil has medium-sized particles; a cross between sandy and clay, it's a good soil to work with. Silty soil has a slightly soapy texture and is usually found in areas near river estuaries. It is considered to be the most fertile soil. It holds a lot of water but, unlike clay, it usually drains well. If you have silty soil that does not drain well, you can add organic matter to improve this.

Pros

- Holds nutrients well
- Needs less watering because it retains moisture
- Most vegetables like silty soil

Cons

- Can become waterlogged
- Can be slippery to work with when wet

Top Tip

Chat with your gardening neighbours. What sort of soil do they have and how do they deal with it?

Acid and Alkaline Soils

As well as understanding the texture of your soil, you'll need to know whether it is acid or alkaline. This is determined by the pH of your soil: pH 7 is neutral; a pH of between 1 and 7 is acid; a pH of between 7 and 14 is alkaline. Most vegetables grow best on slightly acid soil of around pH 6.5 and most garden soils have a pH of between 5 and 9. You can determine the pH of your soil by purchasing a simple soil test kit from a garden centre. Alternatively, you can send a sample to a laboratory for testing. If your soil is very acidic, you can make it more alkaline by mixing garden lime into it.

Designing Your Vegetable Garden

Now you've worked out how much space you have to grow your own food, where the best place is to capture the most light and the condition of your soil, you can begin to plan your garden. First, make a list of everything you think you would like to grow and then check to see which of these plants will thrive in the soil, light and space conditions you have.

Siting the Plot

Keep your vegetable plot convenient. Everyone starts off with enthusiastic ideas but, if you have to walk across muddy ground or need to carry a heavy watering can of water a long way for instance, the novelty might soon wear off. Make sure you have easy access to water at all times and your vegetable garden is somewhere you can easily pop to in order to check up on things and gather items to eat. Working on a flat surface is easier than a slope, so bear this in mind when planning your vegetable garden.

Top Tip

Start too small rather than too confident in a small space and then you can expand your interest and experience.

Crop Rotation

For best results you will need to rotate your crops, or in other words to grow different types of plants in the same area each year. This helps to prevent pests and diseases and stops nutrient depletion in the soil. Rotating crops helps to keep valuable nutrients in the soil. By following one crop with a different type, you can replenish the soil. For example, beans and peas (legumes) fix nitrogen into the soil, so you follow the following year with crops that like lots of nitrogen such as brassicas.

A Simple Three-Year Crop Rotation

▶ Root crops, such as potatoes and onions
▶ Legumes and salad crops, such as beans, peas and lettuce
▶ Brassicas, such as cauliflower and cabbages

Crop Rotation for a Larger Plot

If you have a large plot, a four- or five-part rotation can work even better. A four-part rotation consists of:

▶ Root crops
▶ Potatoes
▶ Legumes
▶ Brassicas

For a five-yearly rotation, follow the same plan but leave one bed fallow for a year, replenishing it with green manure.

Top Tip

You don't have to have separate beds to set up a rotation system. You can rotate in the smallest of spaces or on raised beds.

Allotments and Shared Plots

Most countries have schemes that allow the use or rental of spare land for those who don't have their own garden in which to grow vegetables. There are many benefits to be gained from renting an allotment or shared plot or joining a community gardening project. Not only will you get to meet other people, which turns gardening into a social hobby, but you will also be able to ask other gardeners what works for them and to swap seeds and plants and share your harvest.

Finding an Allotment

Ask your local authority about the availability of allotments, or try your library for advice. Demand is outstripping availability in many areas, so make sure you get your name down on a waiting list straight away if you are considering an allotment. All councils in England and Wales (with the exception of Inner London) legally have to provide allotments for people registered on their electoral roll. In the UK, the current standard plot size for an allotment is 250 m2 (300 sq yds/1⁄16 of an acre), also referred to as 10 pole or rod.

Did You Know?

If you live in the UK and there are no allotments in your area, you can gather a group of six residents registered on your electoral roll and put a case to your local authority to provide them.

Allotment Facilities

The cost of renting an allotment will vary according to the area, demand and facilities. Facilities might include water and/or water butts, car parking, toilets, security and sheds or storage. In some areas, your rent fee will cover nothing but your plot of land. Check out more than one site if you can. Do the allotments look well maintained? Are there signs of damage or vandalism?

Think About Storage

You may be able to erect a shed or other form of storage on your plot. This is worth doing, especially if you have to walk or cycle to your allotment, because it saves you having to carry the right tools with you all the time. You can bet the tool you need is the one you have left at home!

59

Clearing Your Allotment

If you're lucky, you'll inherit an allotment that has been well looked after and all you'll need to do is take over. Many people, however, inherit an overgrown mess that needs clearing. You'll need to dedicate some time and energy into clearing your plot of weeds and overgrowth.

Start by strimming everything near to ground level and then either meticulously dig over and pull out the weeds, or smother the ground with black polythene and leave it for a few weeks for everything to die back. When you remove the plastic, you'll be able to dig the ground more easily, remove seeds and plant roots, leave them to dry in the sun and put them on to the compost heap.

Tackling weeds

It's better for the environment and your health if you avoid toxic weedkillers, but in some instances the ground may be so badly infected with weeds, or you may have so little time on your hands, that you need some quick and effective help. Select a non-residual weedkiller and follow the manufacturer's instructions regarding application and safety guidelines. Leave the weedkiller to take effect for as long as stated on the directions, then dig or rotovate (that is, 'break up using a rotovator') the ground and remove all traces of old plant roots and weeds.

Top Tip

Use old carpet or cardboard sheets to smother weeds. It's a great way to recycle!

Checklist

▶ Determine how much **space** you can dedicate to growing food.

▶ If you're going to grow in containers, start shopping around to see the different **types of containers** available to you.

▶ If you're going to build **raised beds**, think about the materials you might need.

▶ Look into the availability of **'mini' vegetables** – what can you buy and what do you like to eat?

▶ If you're using full-sized beds, do you want to grow neat, uniform rows or do you prefer a **'potager' look**?

▶ Draw a **plan** of your garden to show where the sun falls throughout the day.

▶ Do you need a **polytunnel or greenhouse**? Look at choice and cost.

▶ Buy a soil test kit and check out the **pH of your soil.**

▶ If you want an **allotment,** get your name on a list straight away.

61

What

To Grow

Tasty Choices

One of the most exciting aspects of growing your own vegetables is choosing what to plant. Seed catalogues are full of all sorts of crops that are beautifully photographed and look mouthwatering. Garden centres have racks of exotic-sounding vegetables, all of which are tempting to try.

Plant What You Like

One of the most important questions to ask yourself is 'What do I like to eat?' There is no point spending time and energy in growing something you don't enjoy eating! Wigwams of runner beans look pretty, but they are little use to you if you hate beans. Have a think about your favourite vegetables and herbs and write a list.

Favourite Meals

Think back over the past week or month and make a list of your favourite meals. Were they more traditional, such as a roast dinner with lots of roasted vegetables, or did you cook mainly pasta sauces using tomatoes, onions and peppers? Perhaps you like country garden soups or have a love of mashed swede. What about curries? Root-vegetable curry can be a delicious meal in the winter. Or perhaps you prefer to eat stir-fries, with lots of crunchy vegetables. Maybe you eat salad every day, in which case salad leaves and cucumbers might be better for you to try.

> ## Top Tip
> Keep your shopping receipts for a couple of weeks and look back over them to see what vegetables you regularly buy.

Entertaining

Do you do a lot of entertaining at home? Imagine being able to serve a meal that you have not only cooked yourself, but also grown yourself! You could grow all the ingredients for your favourite starter or main course or you could begin by growing your own herbs to embellish your meals.

Less is More

It's easy to get carried away with ideas, but it's always best to start small. If you try to grow everything you think you want, you'll probably end up with overcrowding, too big a job to take care of and lots of failures. This could put you off for life! It's better to grow one or two containers of something well, than have an allotment you can't bear the thought of visiting. Simply growing five seed potatoes, harvesting your own crop and topping them with some mint butter will be a gastronomic feast that no amount of money can buy.

> ## Top Tip
> Begin by selecting just five different things to grow. This will be rewarding, but your garden will not become a chore.

65

Who is Eating?

Unless you live on your own, it's not just about the meals you eat; you probably also have family or housemates to consider too. Hungry teenagers, weaning babies, inquisitive toddlers, vegetarians, a pregnant mum-to-be, a physically active person, a busy executive, the overweight, the underweight, the infirm and elderly all have different nutritional requirements that you may need to consider when deciding what to grow in your garden.

Pregnant Mothers

A pregnant mum-to-be has a need for a well-balanced diet in order to enjoy a happy and stress-free pregnancy. A wide range of vitamins and minerals are needed to produce a healthy baby, many of which can be obtained from vegetables that you can grow in your garden.

In addition, some gentle gardening is a great activity that can be enjoyed throughout each stage of pregnancy. Obviously you won't want to lift heavy materials or stretch too much, but the gentle stroll around the garden combined with a little stretching can be very beneficial. Gardening can help reduce stress levels too, and provide some moments of solitude.

Weaning Babies

What better way to introduce your baby to solid food than puréed vegetables made from your own garden? Think of the money and waste you will save by doing this yourself rather than buying individual jars of baby food. You'll have no glass jars to dispose of and your baby's carbon footprint will be as tiny as its own feet! No food miles for him or her!

Good Vegetables to Purée

You can purée all sorts of vegetables, except the really fibrous ones. Potatoes and carrots are a great weaning food, parsnips are naturally sweet, and home-grown peas and sweetcorn are more tender than shop bought ones.

Toddlers

Toddlers are ready to explore more textures and some will enjoy going out into the garden to pick their own foods. Raw peas and tiny cherry tomatoes are perfect for little hands and mouths to explore. They will also enjoy the stronger tastes that result from adding herbs to meals, for example basil with tomatoes in a pasta sauce, oregano in casseroles or coriander in a mild curry.

Toddlers like to get their hands into everything, so provide vegetable finger foods, such as cut-up strips of carrot or pepper, and give them portions of whatever you are eating so that they get used to a wide variety of tastes. Coleslaw made from grated carrot, white cabbage and beetroot – all home-grown of course – is a favourite with some toddlers.

School-age Children

By the time a child gets to school age, he or she will hopefully be eating 'adult' meals. There really is no need for separate 'children's food'. You can pack a healthy lunchbox with ingredients from your garden, such as small tomatoes, cucumber, carrot sticks and radishes, and garnish sandwiches with a mixture of salad leaves and herbs. At family mealtimes, children can join you with whatever you are eating. Providing cooked vegetables separately on the table is a good way to allow children to choose what they like and it avoids food waste. If your children go through a phase of not wanting to try vegetables, then try offering them a smooth soup with lots of healthy vegetables in it.

Top Tip

Give your children a small plot of garden to take care of. They can discover the rewards of growing their own food and eating it.

Teenagers

Teenagers can sometimes get into bad eating habits through increased peer pressure. As long as you ensure they have a good breakfast and a healthy meal in the evening, a few chips at lunchtime or occasionally skipping a meal won't do them too much harm.

Tips for Teenagers

▶ **Speed:** Most teenagers don't want to be around their parents much, so think about growing things that can be made into quick meals.

▶ **Accessibility:** Batch cook healthy food and store it in the freezer so that your teens can help themselves to a decent meal at any time of day or night.

▶ **Snacks:** Keep some chopped vegetables ready in the fridge, along with a selection of dips, for when hunger strikes between meals.

▶ **Gentle persuasion:** Try to encourage participation in the family garden if you can, but don't add to the pressure teenagers are already under from friends.

Top Tip

Choose a time to cook and freeze large quantities of pasta sauces, soups and casseroles. You'll always have healthy, 'convenience food' on hand.

Busy Executives

Many people work long hours and barely have time to sit down, let alone eat a meal. Millions of people go to work on an empty stomach and grab something on the run later. If you don't start the day with a good meal, your blood sugar can drop, which leads to cravings. More often than not, the cravings are for sugar, fat, salt or caffeine – hence the coffee and a cake at 11 am!

Thinking about taking care of a garden and preparing food can be just one more thing to add to a full schedule, but your wellbeing will improve if you can spend some time nurturing a garden and yourself. Grow some salad in a window box, and a tomato plant in a container for instant fast food.

The Physically Active

People who have physically demanding lifestyles have different nutritional needs. You'll need protein and carbohydrates, but also lots of vitamins and trace minerals to keep your immune system strong and healthy. You can grow your own carbohydrate-rich foods such as potatoes, parsnips and carrots. For vitamins and minerals, just take your pick of your favourite vegetables! Add any vegetables to hearty soups, casseroles or stir-fries. Taking care of a garden should be no problem if you're used to being active. Maybe the slower pace will be just what you need after a busy day.

The Elderly

Elderly people often have smaller appetites, but need a wide variety of foods to maintain their health. If you yourself are in later life, you may have more time on your hands to experiment with growing heirloom varieties and enjoy cooking more exotic meals. Healthy meals based around vegetables will provide an elderly person who is sedentary with the nutrients that he or she needs.

Top Tip

A meal begins with the sight and smell of food: make meals visually appealing with lots of colour and garnis with herbs for delicate scents.

Convalescence

Perhaps you are getting over an illness yourself, or are taking care of someone who is sick. Fresh food from the garden will give your immune system a powerful boost and the more raw food you can manage, the better. Raw food is lighter on your stomach and no nutrients are lost through cooking. If it seems like too much work to munch through salad items or carrot sticks, then make simple soups and blend them. That way you retain more vitamins and minerals than if you simply boil vegetables then pour the water down the sink. Use a slow cooker or steamer to cook food: it's less washing up and meals can take care of themselves while you rest.

Weight Management

Vegetables are every dieter's friend. If you want to lose weight, then replace unhealthy snacks and meals with lots of fresh fruit, vegetables and salads. Choose varieties of vegetables you enjoy eating and grow them yourself. Not only will you benefit from the exercise involved in gardening, but you'll also enjoy eating fresh vegetables even more if you've grown them yourself.

If you are trying to put on weight, you need to do this in a healthy way, not by eating more fat and sugar! Stocking up on hearty soups, roasted vegetables and rich casseroles will help you increase your weight sensibly.

Top Tip

Grow crops from each colour group. Put these on a plate and you have all the vitamins and minerals you need for one meal!

Seasonal Eating

One of the wonderful things about growing your own vegetables is that you can eat in tune with the seasons. Fifty years ago, we did not expect to eat the same foods all year round. We learned to live in harmony with nature and knew the art of preserving food to see us through the leaner months.

Spring

In the springtime, salad leaves start to appear and the first of the beans and peas ripen. However, a spring day on which it feels like summer is on the way can be followed the next by one that feels like winter again! Nature provides the perfect foods for these abrupt changes in temperature. Salad leaves start to shoot ready to cleanse and detox your system, but there are also filling foods such as broad beans and peas that provide valuable proteins and carbohydrates. Light, cleansing herbs such as chives and marjoram sprout again to help our bodies reawaken after winter.

Summer

The advent of summer sees the arrival of lighter, more watery vegetables such as tomatoes and courgettes. These are satisfying to eat but light to digest. Along with them come cucumbers and more salad leaves, which seem to grow as quickly as you can pick them. Sun-loving herbs are at their peak: these include basil, the perfect partner for tomatoes, and fennel, with its bright yellow flowers. There's not much time to preserve crops; everything grows so fast and demands to be eaten at its best.

Top Tip

Look for a recipe book that provides seasonal recipes and plan some of your vegetable growing around your favourite meals.

Autumn

Autumn is the traditional harvest time. The days are getting shorter and the temperatures are cooler. Along come warming foods with delicious colours to lift your mood. Pumpkins and squashes of all varieties, which ripen in autumn, can be stored for use throughout the winter. Root vegetables can be taken up, dried and stored. A meal of roasted carrots, beetroot, onions and parsnips provides the colours of an autumn sunset on a plate – fiery, warm and comforting.

Winter

During the winter, the soil remains dormant and our bodies feel like doing the same! Fortunately, the foods that remain in the ground and the ones that have been stored are warming and filling. Leeks provide a creamy, rich base for soups, while Brussels sprouts will dutifully

Did You Know?

There are different types of cabbage for all seasons of the year.

stand in the garden waiting to be picked. Thyme and sage will provide you with leaves throughout the season and are perfect for boosting the immune system, fighting infections and improving circulation. Add them to your meals on a regular basis, along with some garlic, and you've got the perfect winter tonic.

Choosing What to Plant Where

Now you know how much space you can use for growing your own food, you can make a more informed choice about which crops you are going to grow where. The secret to success is to allow more room than you think: don't overcrowd the plants. Each one needs space to spread its leaves and roots as well as light, water and nutrients.

Windowsills

It is possible to grow your own food on the windowsills of your home. Bay windows are especially good! All you need is a decent amount of sunlight throughout the day, so walk through each room of the house at different times of the day and make a note of the sunniest spots.

Crops for Windowsills

▶ Chillies
▶ Cherry tomatoes
▶ Small, sweet peppers
▶ Small aubergines
▶ Dwarf French beans

▶ Cut-and-come-again salad leaves
▶ Most herbs, especially basil
▶ Small cucumbers
▶ Rocket
▶ Spring onions

Top Tip

You can make window boxes from recycled materials such as old pallets or offcuts of wood.

Window Boxes

You can grow food in outdoor window boxes too, but make sure they are well secured, particularly if upstairs, and ensure you have easy access to the boxes for watering as they will dry out quickly. Again, make a note of the window ledges that get the most sunlight.

Crops for Window Boxes

▶ Radishes
▶ Baby beetroot
▶ Rainbow chard
▶ Mini spinach
▶ Cut-and-come-again salad leaves
▶ Tomatoes
▶ Courgettes (only one per pot!)
▶ New potatoes (again, one per pot)
▶ Small cabbages
▶ Most herbs, especially rosemary and thyme
▶ Tumbling tomatoes

Hanging Baskets

If your growing space is limited to hanging baskets, you can still enjoy a taste of the good life. Hanging baskets have an advantage over other containers in that they're less likely to be attacked by rampaging slugs (although they may still find a way to climb up if something is tasty enough!). You will need to be vigilant with watering hanging baskets, so look at where you can save water in your home for this. You could siphon off some bath water or shower with a bucket to catch the waste water, for example.

Crops for Hanging Baskets

▶ Tumbling tomatoes

▶ Edible flowers, such as nasturtiums

▶ Most herbs, especially parsley

▶ Mini cucumbers

▶ Beans and peas, which can be left to clamber over the sides

▶ Chillies

Containers

If you have a patio or balcony, you can grow your crops in containers. This gives you more freedom because you can choose the size of your container. All but the biggest and hungriest plants can be grown in suitable containers, but it's best to stick to miniature vegetable varieties initially, along with a selection of herbs.

Top Tip

Save suitable materials, such as polystyrene chips or old broken crocs, to use in pots for drainage.

Crops for Containers

▶ Tomatoes
▶ Courgettes
▶ Runner beans
▶ Carrots
▶ Beetroot and radishes
▶ Cucumbers
▶ Salad leaves (grow in a long trough)
▶ Kale and spinach
▶ Salad onions
▶ Potatoes (great to grow in a stack of tyres)
▶ Most herbs
▶ Mini cauliflower and cabbage
▶ Broad beans

Raised Beds

The optimum size for a raised bed is one that allows you to reach into the centre of the bed without having to step on it, so roughly 90 cm (3 ft). This makes it more accessible for you and prevents you needing to step on the soil, which compacts it. Nearly all vegetables can be grown in a raised bed but, because the soil is shallow, it's not brilliant for climbing plants such as beans, because the depth of soil cannot support the stakes. It is possible to grow potatoes in a raised bed but some can be lost because you can't earth them up very well. As long as the raised bed is deep enough (about 30 cm/12 in), other root vegetables such as carrots and beetroot will do well.

Crops for Raised Beds

- Lettuce and salad leaves
- Radishes
- Onions
- Herbs
- Cucumbers – plant these around the edges to trail down the sides

- Carrots
- Beetroot
- Peas
- Broad beans
- Mini kale

Top Tip

The optimum size for a raised bed is 3 m (10 ft) long by 90 cm (3 ft) wide. This means you won't have to step on to it.

Plants for Garden Beds and Allotments

If you have whole garden beds or an allotment to play with, you can grow whatever you choose! You are limited only by the space you have and the time and energy you can give to your project. It is a good idea to start small, however. Try growing just half a dozen or so crops to begin with, so that you can get a feel for the amount of harvest you get in proportion to the amount of time you have put into growing the crop. Once you have one season's experience, you can expand the following year if you wish.

Crops for Bigger Spaces

- Potatoes
- Tomatoes
- Lettuce
- Radishes
- Onion sets

- Runner beans
- Peas
- Courgettes
- Salad leaves
- Beetroot

The Conditions of Your Plot

By now you will have noted how much sunlight your chosen plot receives and the texture and pH of your soil and whether it has a tendency to become waterlogged or whether drought is likely to be more of a problem. Look at the back of any seed packet and you will find information on the amount of water and sunshine the plants require, which you will need to match to the conditions you have.

Crops for Sunny Spots

Some people are lucky enough to have a sunny patch. The following are sun worshippers, so would love a full sunny site:

▶ Tomatoes
▶ Peppers
▶ Aubergines
▶ Squashes
▶ Sweetcorn
▶ Herbs such as basil, rosemary and thyme

Crops for Partial Shade

Other gardeners have to make do with partial shade. Here are some vegetables and herbs suitable for partial shade and slightly cooler temperatures:

- Spring cabbage
- Broad beans
- Cut-and-come-again salad leaves
- Beetroot
- Kale

- Radishes
- Spinach
- Peas
- Herbs such as chives, mint and parsley

Water Requirements

Some plots tend to get waterlogged or have very good access to water. Others get very dry and access to water is poor. Knowing which vegetables can manage wet conditions and which can tolerate a bit of drought is helpful.

Crops Needing Lots of Water

- Tomatoes
- Cucumbers
- Runner beans (with too little water they will become tough and stringy)

Crops with Lower Water Requirements

- Kale
- Broad beans
- Peas
- Pumpkins
- Brussels sprouts
- Chives

Crops with the Lowest Water Requirements

- Most root crops, such as potatoes, radishes, beetroot and onions
- Herbs such as thyme

Conserving Water

One of the best things you can do with current climate changes is to conserve water wherever possible. Here are some water-saving tips:

- Water plants early in the morning or late at night to reduce evaporation
- Install a couple of water butts to store rainwater
- Mulch around crops to prevent evaporation from the soil
- Remember that containers generally need more watering than beds
- Capture as much water as you can, for example from washing up and baths

81

- Keep soil in good condition, with good moisture-retaining capacity, by adding organic matter
- Set up a drip irrigation system by recycling old plastic bottles
- Select more drought-resistant plants unless your soil is quite damp
- Water plants close to the ground and stem; don't waste it over the leaves

Did You Know?

It is better to give plants a good soaking once or twice a week rather than little and often, or they may develop weak roots.

Acid and Alkaline Soils

By now you should know whether your soil is acid or alkaline. Most plants prefer slightly acidic soil but, unless you have very acid or very alkaline soil, you should be able to grow most things.

Acid-tolerant Plants

If your soil is particularly acid, you could try the following crops before planting other vegetables to see how easy they are to grow:

- Aubergines
- Potatoes

Alkaline-tolerant Plants

If your soil is particularly alkaline, you are likely to have the most success with the following vegetables:

- Cabbages
- Cauliflowers
- Cucumbers
- Beetroot
- Carrots
- Leeks

Soil Texture

You'll also have a good idea about the texture of your soil by now. Is it more sandy or clay based? Loamy soil is ideal, but not many people are fortunate enough to have it!

Crops for Sandy Soil

Root vegetables, such as carrots, radishes, beetroot and garlic, tend to do well in sandy soil because they don't need too much water, plus they can push down easily into the soil. You'll find that salad potatoes are good too. Crops that require a lot of water or food don't tend to do so well in sandy soil because it drains too quickly. Until you have more experience, it would be best to steer clear of vegetables like beans, cabbages and broccoli.

Crops for Clay Soil

Clay soil retains nutrients and water well but it can be difficult for seeds to put down roots or for seedlings to push through clay soil. Root crops such as parsnips and carrots have a

difficult time in clay soil. At best they will 'fork', but often they don't grow more than a couple of centimetres! Salad leaves are a bit tender for heavy clay soils, but you can try planting them later in the season once the soil has warmed up and dried out. Potatoes are great for clay soil as they actually help to break it up. Beans and peas, which often need more water to swell the pods, can do really well in clay soil.

Top Tip

Take a look through your weekly household waste and see what you could divert from landfill to compost heap.

85

Time, Energy and Money

Be realistic: you might have aspirations of being completely self-sufficient, but if you work long hours, have a family to take care of or have other time commitments, you'll need to be honest with yourself about how much time you'll really have available for gardening as this will affect your growing choices. Your energy and skill levels are relevant too – here you will learn which crops are good for beginners. And last but not least, if you want to save money by growing your own veg, there are some crops that are more appropriate.

Gardening in a Few Minutes Per Day

If you choose to grow vegetables and herbs on a windowsill or in hanging baskets, then your gardening

Top Tip

Write a plan of your weekly commitments and look at how much time you could dedicate to gardening.

might take you only a few minutes every day. You'll need to water plants frequently, check them for pests and diseases, feed them when needed and harvest regularly to ensure an ongoing crop. You'll need to sow successionally as well: when you pull up a crop, pop another couple of seeds in its place; or sow a few seeds every week for a continual harvest. If you're not at home much or eat out a lot, then this could be the ideal solution for you.

Containers

If you're going to grow crops in containers on a patio or balcony, it will take a little more time. Perhaps ten minutes per day. You'll need to ensure frequent watering, particularly during dry spells, you might need to turn containers to get even sunlight and you'll need to pick crops regularly to keep them productive. The amount of time you spend container gardening will depend on the number of pots you have and the requirements of your crops. Tomatoes, for example, like a lot of water and regular feeding, whereas carrots will more or less take care of themselves.

Gardening for Those With More Time

You won't need a lot of time even for growing your own vegetables in raised beds – perhaps an hour or so a week, depending on how many you have. Larger beds and allotments require more care and attention – up to several hours a week. You'll need to be vigilant about crop rotation, weeding will take longer and you'll have more crops to take care of. Some may get pests and diseases, which will need to be treated to prevent them spreading. There will be more harvesting to do and you'll need more time to preserve your crops if you get a glut. In addition, the soil will need more care at the beginning and end of each season. The upside is that you'll have more food to eat and save more money in the long run!

Ten Good Crops for Beginners

Some crops are easier to take care of than others. If you can be vigilant about watering and feeding, tomatoes are easy to grow and many herbs will take care of themselves. Other than these, the easiest to grow include:

▶ Beetroot   ▶ Potatoes
▶ Broad beans   ▶ Radishes
▶ Courgettes   ▶ Runner beans
▶ Dwarf beans   ▶ Salad leaves
▶ Onions   ▶ Spinach

Value for Money

Potatoes, runner beans, courgettes and tomatoes should provide you with a huge harvest, giving great savings. Bags of salad and spinach cost a lot to buy in the supermarket and often half of it gets thrown away because you can't eat it in time, so grow your own to save money. Although onions are cheap to buy, many people use so many of them it is worth growing your own so that you don't run out at that crucial time!

Top Tip

Putting containers on castors makes it easier to move things around.

88

Checklist

▶ Look at what vegetables or herbs you would need for your **favourite meal** and see how many of them you could grow.

▶ Work out how big a plot you need based on **how many people** you cook for each day.

▶ Select just five crops to grow to **avoid overstretching** yourself.

▶ Start saving **old jars with lids** for making chutneys and pickles.

▶ Get into the habit of **batch cooking** to create instant healthy 'convenience' food.

▶ Decide how much **space** you have to grow food and think what **containers** you might need.

▶ See if you can make window boxes or raised beds from **materials in your garage or shed.**

▶ Compare your **soil type** to some vegetable requirements and see which will work best in your plot.

▶ Read the list of **crops for beginners** and choose your favourites.

Preparing To Grow

Planning Your Plot

The design of your garden will depend a lot on the space you have. If you're going to grow food in hanging baskets or containers or on windowsills, you'll need to be creative with space to maximize your yield, but you'll also need to ensure you have space to reach and water them all. If you have raised beds, traditional garden beds or an allotment, you will have more space to grow larger crops but you'll still need to make sure you can maintain them.

Planning for Tender Plants

Some plants are more tender than others. Some will 'sulk' if they aren't watered for a day, may topple over easily, need protecting from frosts or will scorch in strong sunlight. If you are planning to grow crops that might get blown over in a strong wind, such as tall wigwams of runner beans, then you'll need to plan for their protection. If you intend to grow plants that need a lot of water, you'll need to make sure you have a handy water supply.

Grouping Plants

Plan your garden so that you can work as efficiently as possible. It makes sense to group plants that have similar requirements. For example, put all your hungry feeders together. This will make it easier for you to maintain your garden and will reduce the chance

Top Tip

Use graph paper to make a to-scale plan of your garden.

of you forgetting to feed the odd tomato plant at the end of your plot. Remember that you'll be rotating your crops on a yearly basis for best results, so plan ahead and consider whether this will be practical in your chosen garden design.

Good Design

A well-designed vegetable garden is easy to maintain. The containers or beds will be easily accessible; you won't have to traipse over muddy paths or step on your beds and you will be able to reach pots at the back. Make sure hanging baskets are not too high for you to water, as you'll have to do this twice a day in dry weather. Make sure your tools are readily available; you don't want to keep walking through your house to find a pair of gloves, for example. Set up a good water supply, organize a container for putting weeds into and make a compost heap. If you make your garden a pleasure to work in, you'll be more likely to spend time tending to it.

Practical Design

You'll probably want your gardening space as close to the kitchen as possible. Put your favourite herbs close to the back door or grow some small pots on your kitchen windowsill. Cut-and-come-again salad leaves, which require constant picking, and tomatoes or runner beans, which ripen overnight, are more likely to provide you with a continual crop if they are handy for you to reach. Crops that can be left for longer, such as potatoes, can be planted further from your house because they don't require so much attention.

Did You Know?

Basil and tomatoes are traditional 'companion' plants. Plant them together to improve the taste of your tomatoes.

Windy Conditions

Some gardens suffer from driving winds, which can damage plants. If your vegetable garden is in a very windy area, you'll need to deal with the problem to prevent losing your crops, as not many plants will tolerate such extreme conditions. Growing vegetables in windy conditions usually means your crops will take longer to establish themselves and start growing. In addition, the wind will dry out the soil more quickly and your plants will lose more water by transpiration, which means you need to keep an eye on their water requirements.

Wind Protection

Plants growing in an exposed situation will need more protection than those in a more sheltered spot, so make provision for this before beginning to grow anything. High-level balconies and exposed gardens can be particularly affected by wind, so you'll need to build structures to redirect the gusts. Strong trellises and permeable fencing are ideal, and they can double up as structures to grow vegetables against. If you have room, you could plant hedges or shrubs to filter wind, but make sure that they do not create too much shading. Hedges have the added advantage of attracting beneficial wildlife to your

Did you know?

Hedges and shrubs in your garden can attract hedgehogs, which will eat some of the slugs in your garden.

garden. Protecting seedlings with cloches or fleece is more challenging because they can blow away if not securely fixed.

Suitable Windbreaks

Suitable windbreaks include strong trellises, open-style fencing, hedges and shrubs. Structures such as solid walls and closed panel fencing are not good choices. A solid structure will simply cause turbulence, which can do just as much harm to your plants

95

Top Tip

If you are growing in containers, you can turn them to make the most of sunlight.

and not improve the situation at all. With a solid windbreak such as a wall, the wind rushes over the top and gets pulled down the other side, where it swirls around, a bit like a current in a stream. With a more open structure, the wind is diffused through the gaps.

Sunlight

Most plants need six to eight hours of sunlight to grow well. When plants have to compete for light, they become weaker, which can make them more prone to disease and vulnerable to attack by pests. Some shading can be dealt with, by pruning a

Did You Know?

Mint repels cabbage flies, so plant containers of mint among your cabbages.

hedge or tree, for example. But a little more work may be required, for example moving a shrub to a more suitable location. Be aware that if you live in a conservation area, you may need permission to do this.

Getting More Sun

If you cannot get more sun on to your plot because the structures creating the shade are immovable (such as a building) or do not belong to you (a neighbour's favourite tree), then you'll either have to consider creating your plot somewhere else or simply have a go and see what you can do with the conditions you have. With dappled sunlight or sun for part of the day, you may manage to grow things that take a little longer to mature or do not have such big crops. Sometimes this is a blessing, especially with courgettes, which can turn into marrows overnight!

Cool Shade

There are some plants, such as salad leaves and spinach, that do well in a cooler, more shaded situation. Generally plants with big green leaves will grow well with less sunlight, much better than plants that need to set fruit, such as tomatoes.

You'll also find that some herbs, including mint and parsley, do well in shadier conditions. Often plants will bolt if they get too hot; this is especially true of spinach and salad leaves. So turn your shady spot into an advantage. Remember: gardening is all about co-operating with nature and making the most of what you have!

97

Preparing Your Ground

Preparing your ground properly is very important. In order to have healthy plants, you need healthy, fertile soil. Your crop will only be as good as the soil you plant it in. There are ways to improve the condition and texture of your soil to increase nutrients and improve absorbency of water, and there are ways to enrich your soil so that it provides the perfect growing medium for your plants.

When to Prepare Your Soil

The best time for preparing your soil is autumn or springtime, but don't worry about this if you are new to gardening and want to get out there and try something. It's never the wrong time of year to pull up a weed or tidy the ground. Indeed, it's better to get outside and do a little bit of gardening than to wait for the perfect day and do nothing at all for a few weeks.

Preparing Clay Soil

If you have clay soil you can't dig it when it is too wet. This can damage the soil structure and prevent it draining properly. It is very hard work digging wet clay in any case! If you stick your fork or spade in the ground and the soil sticks to it, then it's too wet to dig. Leave it to dry out for a few days and try again.

Top Tip

Remember at all times to feed your soil, not the plant. Without healthy soil you won't get healthy plants.

Compaction

You should avoid stepping on your soil wherever possible. Walking on the soil will compact it and can cause structural damage to the surface of the ground. In addition, it makes it more difficult to sow directly into the soil if the top layer is compacted. If you have large beds to take care of, then put a few old planks of wood down to walk on. Be aware that the planks can provide hiding places for slugs. Take the planks off the soil when you have finished with them.

First Steps

The first step to preparing your ground is to remove any obvious waste such as dead flowers, old plants, weeds and roots. Most plants, except tenacious weeds and diseased plants, can be dried and added to your compost heap. Once you have removed all obvious 'rubbish', it's time to improve the texture of the soil so that seeds can put down roots and seedlings can push through the soil easily. You can improve the texture of all types of soil, except peaty, with the addition of lots of organic matter such as well-rotted manure or compost.

Feeding the Soil

Get hold of some well-rotted manure if you can. This is the best way to improve your soil texture. Horse manure is great; you'll get the solids, liquids and straw bedding, which will add structure, break down soil and help your soil to maintain nutrients and water. If you can't get hold of manure, then use good-quality garden compost; either from your own compost heap, or bought from a garden centre.

Top Tip

Ask at a local stable for horse manure; you'll often get it for free if you can collect and bag it yourself.

Well-rotted Manure

It's important to use 'well-rotted', rather than fresh, manure on your garden beds. Well-rotted manure has been composted down, is crumbly in texture and sweet smelling (unlike something that is fresh from the animal). You can sometimes buy well-rotted manure from a farmer or stables, but if you get it fresh, it is easy to rot down yourself as long as you have space to store it. Simply cover it with tarpaulin and leave it for six months.

Compost

Compost can be bought in bags from your local garden centre but, if you have space for it, it is much better to set up your own compost heap as it reduces the amount of waste you send to landfill and will save you a lot of money in the long run. You don't need any special materials; you can simply set up a

Did You Know?

Much of your weekly
household waste, including
junk mail, cardboard
packaging and eggshells,
can be composted.

heap in the corner of your garden. Alternatively, make a compost
bin from old pallets, or buy a ready-made compost bin.

Compost Ingredients

To make compost you need a mix of green and brown ingredients.
Green materials – wetter ingredients such as fruit and vegetable
peelings and grass clippings – are rich in nitrogen and quick to
break down. Brown materials – drier ingredients such as shredded
newspaper, cardboard and straw – are rich in carbon, slower to break down and let air pockets develop in
the compost heap. If you've ever tried to make compost before and ended up with a wet, slimy, smelly mess

it's probably because you put too many 'green' ingredients in and not enough 'browns'. Aim for equal amounts by volume of both types.

What to Compost

Here are 10 things you might not have guessed you could compost!

▶ **Feathers:** If you have feather pillows or duvets that shed their contents, add them to your compost heap.

▶ **Human hair and pet fur:** When you brush your hair or pamper your pet, add the loose hair or fur to your compost pile.

▶ **Human urine:** Male pee is a great compost activator, adding huge amounts of nitrogen to get the decomposition process working.

▶ **Nail clippings:** When you give yourself a manicure, add your nail clippings to the compost heap. (But don't do this if you varnish your nails.)

▶ **Nut shells:** A few added to the compost heap will add valuable nutrients.

▶ **Pond weed:** Clearing out your pond? Add the weed to the compost heap.

▶ **Textiles:** Do you do a lot of sewing, knitting or crafts and have small scraps of textiles and thread to get rid of? If they are

Top Tip

Mix the contents of your compost pile with a garden fork every time you walk past it to keep it aerated.

made from natural materials such as cotton, wool or silk, you can add small amounts to your compost heap.

▶ **Vacuum cleaner contents:** If you have natural flooring, empty your vacuum bag contents into the compost instead of the landfill.

▶ **Vegetarian pet bedding:** Guinea pigs, chickens, rabbits and hamsters provide excellent compost material – throw it in, sawdust and all!

▶ **Wine corks:** Make sure they are real cork and not plastic ones, then chop them up and add them to the mix.

How to Compost

Making compost is a bit like making a cake:

▶ Assemble your ingredients
▶ Mix them together
▶ Bake

The conditions needed for good compost are:

▶ Air
▶ Ingredients
▶ Warmth
▶ Water

Getting the Right Mix

To ensure your compost heap has enough air you need to make sure you put enough browns into it and turn the heap regularly. This will help the composting process by adding warmth to the ingredients. The water comes from a good balance of green to brown ingredients. If you have the right balance, the texture will resemble a well-wrung sponge. Grab a handful of compost from the middle of the pile and see if you can squeeze a couple of drops of moisture from it. If you can, the consistency is right. If it's too dry, you can carefully water the pile or add more green ingredients. If it is too wet, you'll need to add more brown materials to soak up the moisture.

How Long Does it Take?

You can make compost in as little as three months, but by gradually adding ingredients when you get them, mixing them up and allowing them to decompose, it will probably take six months to a year. Finished compost is dark brown or black with a crumbly texture and a sweet smell. It will bear no resemblance to the original ingredients and will have shrunk to half of its original volume. If your compost is not ready, simply pile it back up, mix it again and leave nature to do its work. Never put 'half-cooked' compost on to your soil as it can burn tender plant roots.

Digging it In

Don't skimp on the amount of manure or compost you use. You'll need to use about half a wheelbarrow load per square metre of ground. Empty out the manure or compost on to your ground and start digging it in. This can be hard work on clay soil, but console yourself with the fact that once you have improved the texture of the soil by digging in the organic matter, you will have fertile, nutrient-rich soil. On sandy soil, the digging will be much easier and the addition of organic matter will help the soil to retain moisture and nutrients rather than draining so quickly.

Top Tip

When it comes to digging in compost or manure, do it in short bursts, especially if you are new to gardening.

Trench Digging

There are many schools of thought on how to dig manure and compost into your soil. Here is one of the more traditional methods:

▶ **Clear and dig:** Once you have removed all obvious weeds and plant roots, dig a trench roughly 25 cm (10 in) wide along the length of your bed.

▶ **Layer:** Put a 7–10 cm (3–4 in) layer of organic matter into the bottom of the trench.

▶ **Dig and cover:** Dig another trench parallel to the first one. As you are digging, put the soil you dig out of this second trench over the organic matter in the first trench.

▶ **Layer:** Put a 7–10 cm (3–4 in) layer of organic matter into the bottom of the second trench.

▶ **Dig and cover:** Dig another trench parallel to the first and second trenches and put the soil you dig out of this third trench over the organic matter in the second trench.

▶ **Layer:** Put a 7–10 cm (3–4 in) layer of organic matter into the bottom of the third trench and so on until you have finished the entire bed.

▶ **Cover:** Finish by using the soil dug out of the first trench to cover the organic matter in the final trench.

Making it Easier

If all that trench digging sounds like too much hard work or you are limited by time or physical constraints, try this easier method. It will still get the organic matter into the soil but is less strenuous. Again, you first need to remove all obvious weeds and plant roots, then:

▶ Fork over the first few inches of top soil to break down any lumps of soil.

▶ Spread around 5 cm (2 in) of organic matter over the surface of the soil.

▶ Lightly fork the organic matter into the soil.

No-dig Gardening

There is an even easier way to get organic matter into your soil and that is to put down your spade and let nature do the work for you! Some gardeners believe that digging damages the soil and increases nutrient loss. The idea behind the 'no-dig' method is that instead of annual digging, you apply a thick layer of organic matter to the top of your soil and let the earthworms do everything. You will need a lot of compost or manure for the no-dig method as you spread thick layers of it on top of your soil.

More Advantages of No-dig

No-dig is not suitable for very heavy clay soils and is only viable for beds that you don't need to walk on, so ensure they are small enough before you start. No-dig gardening is not a quick-fix method – it takes a few years of perseverance to get rid of weeds and build up quality soil – but advocates say that the long-term rewards are worth it. Instead of just using manure or compost, you can cover the area with thick sheets of damp cardboard or newspaper and put layers of organic matter, such as manure, compost, leaf mould, straw or spent mushroom compost, on top.

> ## Did You Know?
> Advocates of the no-dig method say it makes the soil more resistant to pest attack.

Using the No-Dig Method

▶ Hoe off any obvious weeds and pick out the roots

▶ Spread at least a 5 cm (2 in) layer of rotted organic matter over the surface of the soil during the autumn

▶ Leave the bed alone for the winter

▶ In the spring, transplant crops straight on to the mulched surface

Pros of No-Dig Gardening

▶ Saves heavy digging

▶ Prevents you compacting the soil by treading on it

▶ Increases the fertility of the soil

▶ Ideal for raised beds

Cons of No-Dig Gardening

▶ Not suitable for very heavy clay soils

▶ You need large quantities of well-rotted organic matter for this method to work

▶ It can be a long time before you see results

Raised Beds

Raised beds, in the form of rectangular or square frames made from wood or bricks that are filled with soil or compost, are the ideal solution for some people. You can make them as high as you wish off the ground as long as you have enough soil with which to fill them.

Making Raised Beds

For each raised bed, you will need enough wood for the frame. You should never walk on the soil of a raised bed, so you need to be able to reach easily into the centre from each side of the bed. This means that the maximum width of the bed will be about 90 cm (3 ft). Don't make the raised bed any longer than 3 m (10 ft) otherwise you will be tempted to walk across it rather than around it! Ensure you leave enough room between beds to walk, kneel or move a wheelbarrow around. Once you have built your frame in situ, ensure it drains well by putting a layer of sand and rock in the bottom. Fill it up with good-quality soil, free of weed seeds, and you're ready to go!

Pros of Raised Beds

- Reported to increase crop yield.
- Warm up quickly so you can get a head start on sowing.
- Easier access – great for those who are unable to bend or need to use wheelchairs.
- Soil can be chosen to match the plants you want to grow.
- Ideal for small gardens – you can design the raised bed to fit your space.
- Generally have fewer weeds than the ground and are easier to maintain.
- Excellent for root crops, such as carrots, which need fine soil to push into, and salad leaves, which need a tilthy (well-tilled) soil.
- Excellent drainage if well-designed and maintained.

Cons of Raised Beds

- High set-up costs – you need wood, a base and lots of good-quality soil that is free of weed seeds.
- It can take some time to put together a raised bed system.
- Ongoing maintenance is required to keep beds in good condition.
- Need more watering than crops planted straight into the earth.
- More limited space – which makes them generally unsuitable for very large crops such as pumpkins.
- Weeding will need doing by hand rather than with a hoe or rotovator.
- You need to buy good-quality wood for the frames otherwise they can rot quickly.
- You also need to make sure that wood has not been treated with anything toxic that might leach into your soil.

Top Tip

Use the best materials you can afford when constructing a raised bed so that it lasts a long time. You can buy kits.

Containers

You might prefer to use, or only have the room for, containers to grow your vegetables. There are many advantages to container gardening: you can choose exactly the right soil for the plants you want to grow, you can position them anywhere handy and move them about at the end of the season and, provided you use the correctly sized containers, you can grow virtually any vegetables except very heavy feeders or large crops.

Choosing Containers

You need to choose containers based on your budget and the plants you want to grow. Spend time thinking about how many different types of vegetable or herb you want and research to see how much space they will take up once fully mature. Buy the best-quality pots you can in the largest size you can afford, but make sure they are not too heavy for you to move about. Larger pots require less watering and maintenance and will hold more nutrients because you can get more soil into them. The minimum-sized pot you will need is around 20 cm (8 in) deep.

Plastic Pots

Plastic pots are the cheapest pots to buy. You can buy them virtually anywhere for a minimal investment. However, they are not so good for the environment and they can break easily; they are prone to UV damage from sunlight and can start to disintegrate after a couple of years. Nevertheless, for a first-time gardener, they are the budget option and will give you the opportunity to find out whether gardening is for you or not. You can move them around easily and they are good for balconies, where there may be a weight restriction.

Clay or Terracotta Pots

These pots are inexpensive, robust enough to stand a wind but not too heavy to move. They keep soil warmer than wooden containers and don't need any maintenance. All terracotta pots are not the same, however, and you'll need to make sure that yours are frost-proof. Unglazed pots will need more watering than those made of other materials because they are porous.

Top Tip
Try Freecycle for some free containers of all shapes and sizes. You are more likely to strike lucky if you ask 'out of season'.

Stone Pots

Stone pots are usually much more expensive and are much heavier than terracotta. Once you have put them in place and filled them with soil, they are there to stay! They are an investment, however, will stand all

weathers and will last for years. They take longer to warm up but retain the heat well once summer comes.

Wooden Containers

Half barrels make very attractive plant containers and you can buy wooden pots that are square. You can also make your own wooden containers from offcuts of wood, which means you can keep your budget down. You will need to choose seasoned wood

Top Tip

Look around your home for suitable 'free' containers such as old saucepans and plastic pots.

otherwise it will swell up and warp when wet. Wooden containers will need maintenance to prevent them going rotten. If you're growing in window boxes, wood is the ideal material for troughs and it looks more attractive than plastic.

Hanging Baskets

Hanging baskets come in a variety of shapes, materials and sizes and need a strong bracket to secure them to a wall. You will also need moisture-retentive material to line the basket and will need to be prepared to water them daily, sometimes twice a day. Hanging baskets can be difficult to maintain because they dry out quickly in heat and wind due to their shallow structure.

Other Containers

You are limited only by your imagination when it comes to suitable containers for gardening. Old Belfast sinks, buckets, bowls and car tyres can all be used and they are only the tip of the iceberg! Look around in other people's gardens and you'll see everything from holey wheelbarrows to shoes, enamel baths to old watering cans, which just goes to show you don't need to spend lots of money to set up a garden.

Preparing Containers

It is vital that all containers have good drainage to prevent your crops rotting. You will need to drill holes in the bottom of each pot, if they are not already there, and put a layer of drainage material, such as stones or gravel, in the base of each one before filling them with soil. Containers can be a breeding ground for diseases, so you need to keep them meticulously clean. At the end of the growing season, empty out the contents and wash the pots with a little washing-up liquid. Leave them to air dry and store them in a cool, dry space until you need them again.

Seeds

Top Tip

Browsing through seed catalogues during the winter gives you time to plan rather than rushing to the garden centre during the spring to make impulsive choices.

Now you've planned your garden and decided what to plant it's time to get some seeds! Seeds are amazing things; inside each one is all the information to grow a plant. Seeds remain dormant, sometimes for years, until germination is triggered by moisture and warmth.

You can buy seeds from garden centres, specialist gardening catalogues or online. Most seed packets will contain a photograph of what is in them, along with the full name and variety, with sowing and planting directions on the back.

Cutting Costs

The chances are that a gardening friend, neighbour or work colleague will have lots of seeds they can donate to you when you're starting out. Ask around and see what people can offer. Another place to ask is Freecycle. You might be able to put up an advert and ask for seeds in return for a share of your crop, or, if you are only going to grow a small number of varieties, you may decide to buy plants from a nursery instead. You'll get far more seeds in a packet than you need in most cases, so think about going halves with a friend. The other thing to do is save your own seeds from your first crop so that you can plant them next year – for free!

Fertilizers

Plants need nutrients to grow and develop into strong, healthy specimens. Fertilizers add nutrition to the soil for your plants to use. Some are spread over or dug into the soil before planting, others are added to the water you are going to use on your crops. There are also foliar feeds, which are sprayed on to the leaves only. If you're new to gardening, it's best to stick to a general 'all-purpose' product that has a slow-release formula. Whether you use pellets or liquids is up to you.

Nutrients

The three main elements in fertilizers are nitrogen for leaf growth, phosphorous for healthy roots and potassium (or potash) for fruits and flowers. You may see these elements referred to as NPK, which matches their chemical symbols. All-purpose fertilizers contain other nutrients and trace elements in varying proportions as well as the main NPK elements.

Top Tip
Make your own natural fertilizers by seeping nettles or comfrey in water to make 'tea'.

Organic or Non-Organic?
You will need to decide at this stage whether you want to use organic or non-organic fertilizer. Non-organic fertilizers are cheap to buy and readily available but some people don't want to use chemicals on their garden. Organic fertilizers are generally more expensive to buy but are made from natural ingredients.

Gardening Tools

The range of gardening tools available is as huge as the choice of pots, seeds and fertilizers. You will find a good selection in garden centres and online, but think carefully first about what you really need.

Choosing Tools

It's tempting to rush out and stock up your potting shed with a gleaming set of tools designed to save you time and effort, but think of gardening tools like kitchen gadgets. How many of those 'must-have' kitchen gadgets are gathering dust somewhere? It is far better to buy one good-quality trowel that fits snugly in your hand, is a pleasure to use and doesn't warp if you hit a stone than to have cheap tools for every job that are uncomfortable and ineffective.

Basic Tools for Container Gardening

If you are going to grow food in hanging baskets, window boxes or containers,
you need very few tools. The minimum requirements might be:

▶ Hand trowel
▶ Watering can
▶ Compost bin (if you have room)

You can make a dibber (for making holes in the soil for your seeds) from an old piece of wood or stick
and you might like a pair of decent gardening gloves too.

Basic Tools for Gardening in Raised Beds

If you are going to be planting in one or more raised beds, you will need a few more tools.
A suggested minimum requirements list is:

▶ Hand trowel
▶ Hand fork
▶ Rake
▶ Watering can
▶ Container for gathering produce and collecting weeds
▶ Water butt (if you have room)
▶ Compost bin (if you have room)

You may also like to add some string, secateurs, gardening
gloves and dibbers.

Did You Know?

Some of the best
gardening tools
are made from
copper. They are more
expensive, but a
pleasure to use.

Additional Tools for Larger Plots

Growing a lot of food doesn't necessarily mean using many more tools, but if you have a larger plot you will probably need to add the following to the recommended tool list for raised bed gardening:

▶ Spade
▶ Long-handled fork
▶ Wheelbarrow
▶ Hoe
▶ Shovel
▶ Hose pipe and water butts

Tool Care

Always clean and dry your tools before putting them away to reduce the risk of spreading disease. Store them in a clean, dry, airy space to stop them going rusty and don't leave them out in the rain! If your tools have wooden handles, oil them with linseed oil once a year to nourish the wood and prevent it drying out. If you have the space, hang your tools on a garage or shed wall so that you can find them easily and they don't get damaged. Keep any blades or cutting edges sharp: if you try to cut plants with blunt implements you could damage them.

Top Tip

Ask around for the loan of tools; you'll be surprised how many people have surplus tools they never use.

Checklist

▶ Write a list of you and your family's **favourite vegetables and herbs** before deciding what to grow.

▶ Write a list of your **favourite meals** to see which vegetables and herbs feature most strongly.

▶ **Less is more** – grow half a dozen crops for your first year and see how you get on.

▶ If you're limited to a **small growing space**, choose suitable crops such as mini vegetables, salad leaves and herbs.

▶ If you have a **sunny site** you could try tomatoes, peppers and sweetcorn.

▶ If your site is **shaded**, salad leaves, kale and cabbages will grow well.

▶ **Thirsty crops** include tomatoes, cucumbers and runner beans.

▶ Crops with **less need for water** include kale, broad beans and Brussels sprouts.

▶ Some crops with the **least water requirements** include root crops and many herbs.

How
To Grow

Preparing the Soil for Sowing

One of the first jobs in spring is to prepare your beds for sowing by creating a fine tilth. Tilthy soil is fine and crumbly, a bit like breadcrumbs, with no stones, clods or lumps. If your soil is uneven or lumpy you won't be able to plant straight rows and each seed will be at a different depth, which could result in patchy germination. Some seeds will not germinate because they won't be able to send down roots or push their shoots through the earth.

Creating a Fine Tilth

How much work you will have to do will depend on the texture of your soil, how much you were able to do in the autumn and what the winter weather conditions were like. Lots of winter frosts help to break down the soil, but if it's been a warm, damp winter you may have more work to do in the spring.

Top Tip

If you have heavy clay soil, cover the surface with cloches during the winter to keep the soil warmer and drier for you to work on during the spring.

Five Steps for a Fine Tilth

▶ **Check soil condition:** If it's too wet, i.e. if it sticks to your boots, don't work on it.

122

▶ **Break down:** Once the soil is dry enough, break down any clods with a fork, working quickly and lightly.

▶ **First sweep:** Remove any stones and obvious rubbish from the surface of the soil.

Top Tip

Good soil preparation can make a big difference to successful germination.

▶ **Second sweep:** Rake the surface of the soil lightly to remove more stones, weed roots and break down any lumps. If you have good soil anyway, then you might be able to skip straight to raking the surface of the soil without any need for previous preparation.

▶ **Third sweep:** Keep working until your soil resembles fine breadcrumbs and has an even surface.

Sowing Seeds

Now you've prepared your soil to a fine tilth you're ready to sow. You can choose whether to sow directly outdoors, which is the most traditional method, or sow indoors and transplant your seedlings later on. There are advantages to both, depending on your weather conditions and what you are growing. Some seedlings don't like to be moved and are therefore best planted in situ, while others prefer to be kept protected until they are more established.

When to Sow

Most seed sowing is done in the spring, but seed packets bought from a garden centre will show you sowing times along with transplanting and harvesting

Top Tip

Seeds should be sown at the depth of their own length for best results.

124

times. The temptation will be to rush out on the first warm spring day and throw some seeds in the soil. However, plenty of gardeners have lost their crop to late frosts, so beware of being too hasty. It's better to wait and be successful than sow too early and lose the lot.

Top Tip

When sowing directly outdoors, make sure your soil is damp before you put the seeds in. Water the soil beforehand if you need to.

How Deep to Sow

Some seeds, such as carrot or basil seeds, are tiny and delicate; others, such as runner bean seeds, are larger and more robust. Generally, the finer the seed the less deeply it should be sown. One mistake many gardeners make is to sow too deeply, with the result that the seeds run out of energy before they can push through the soil and they fail to germinate.

Sowing Outdoors

The most traditional method of sowing seeds is in rows along the length of your beds. This is fine if you want a large crop and can cope with a glut. However, not many people can cope with an entire row of lettuces coming up at once. Crops that can be preserved, such as runner beans, are easier to grow in long rows, as you can freeze the surplus produce. If your rows are long, it's a good idea to mark them out with a piece of string to get straight rows. Make a drill, which is basically a tiny trench, to the depth you want to sow your seeds, and place the seeds as evenly as you can along the length of the drill. Seed packets will tell you how closely to sow them. Cover the seeds with a thin layer of soil and water.

125

Sowing Tiny Seeds

Tiny seeds are more difficult to handle than others. Tip some of the seeds into the palm of your hand and sprinkle a few from between your forefinger and thumb, much like you would sprinkle salt on to your food. Alternatively, put the seeds into a seed dispenser, which can be bought from garden centres or made yourself. Don't worry too much about fine sowing at this stage, though; small seeds, such as lettuces and carrots, can be thinned out later once the seedlings appear.

Top Tip

Mix very fine seeds such as carrot with a bit of horticultural sand to make sowing easier.

Sowing Larger Seeds

Mid-sized seeds, such as beetroot, are much easier to handle. Plant two or three in the same place and take out the weakest two plants once the seedlings begin to grow. For larger seeds, such as peas and runner beans, you don't need to make a drill; you can simply push them down in the soil to the right depth with your finger. Once you've sown your seeds, carefully cover them with sieved soil and water them. Remember not to sow them too deeply.

Top Tip

Prepare your seed bed a month before you plan to sow. When the first weeds come up, remove them carefully with a hoe and then sow your seeds to prevent them competing with weeds for nutrients.

Seed Tapes

If you find handling tiny seeds difficult then seed tapes may be the answer. Seed tapes are made from biodegradable material that is impregnated with seeds at regular intervals.

They are ideal for beginners, those who find handling tiny seeds a challenge, the visually impaired who find it hard to see tiny seeds, those who find thinning out difficult or people who are short of time. Tapes are ideal if you want to sow in drills: simply make your drill, put the seed tape into it, cover with soil, water and wait for your seedlings to grow.

Top Tip

Cover tiny seeds with a fine layer of sieved compost. This should prevent you sowing them too deeply and will show you where you have planted them.

Seed Mats

Seed mats are similar to seed tapes but more suitable if you are not planting in rows – for using in containers, for example. Made from biodegradable material and pre-sown with seeds, the mats can be placed in a container or on a plot of land, watered, covered and left. You don't need to thin out or handle tiny seeds and they can save you a lot of time if you are busy. You'll find seed mats and tapes at garden centres or you can buy them online.

Indoor Sowing

You might prefer to start your seeds off indoors, in a greenhouse or windowsill. Some plants, such as courgettes, squash and tomatoes, prefer the protection of being grown indoors and don't mind being transplanted. Check seed packets for advice.

How to Plant Seeds Indoors

▶ **Compost:** Use a seed tray, or small plant pot for each seed. Fill each container with damp seed compost, watering it if it is too dry.

▶ **Sow:** Sprinkle seeds over the compost and cover with a fine layer of sieved compost. (Remember to sow your seeds only as deep as their own length.)

▶ **Protect:** Cover the pots with a sheet of clear plastic or glass or wrap loosely in clear plastic bags.

▶ **Check:** Pots and seed trays dry out more quickly than large areas of soil, so do a daily check and make sure the compost is kept moist.

▶ **Reveal:** Once the seeds start to germinate, remove the plastic or glass, otherwise it may encourage disease.

Top Tip

If you grow your seedlings on your windowsill, turn them regularly so they don't grow lopsided in search of light.

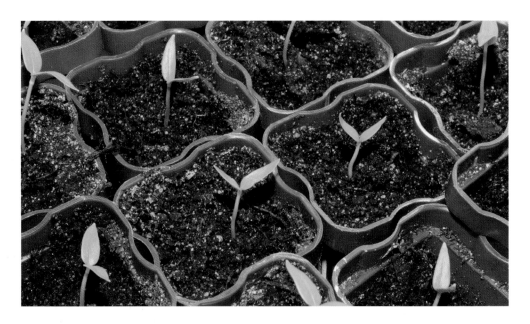

Caring for Seedlings

Once your seedlings have started to grow you need to take good care of them. After four to six weeks they will be large enough to be pricked out and transplanted into a larger pot. After a further couple of weeks, they can be hardened off and planted outdoors or moved to their final growing pots.

Damping Off

One of the worst things to strike young seedlings is damping off. Damping off is caused by a fungus that can affect both indoor – and outdoor – sown seeds, and it will kill your seedlings. The best advice is to take precautionary measures to prevent it happening in the first place.

Tips for Avoiding Damping Off

▶ Use fresh seed compost when sowing seeds.

▶ Wash and disinfect all pots, trays and any other tools, such as dibbers.

▶ Ensure good drainage in your containers.

▶ Use clean fresh water – not stagnant water that has been around a while.

▶ Sow thinly, and thin or prick out before seedlings become overcrowded

▶ Keep temperatures constant; cold draughts and cold wet soil can kill seedlings

▶ Ensure there is good air circulation around your seedlings

▶ Keep conditions well ventilated; humidity adds to the risk of damping off

▶ Natural remedies include weak chamomile tea and cinnamon powder

Pricking Out

Once your seedlings have developed two sets of leaves they need to be moved to give them space to grow into strong, healthy plants. If you initially sowed your seeds in individual pots, you can skip this step. But if you scattered them into a container and the seedlings are getting crowded, you will need to prick them out. Pricking out simply means moving seedlings to give them room to put down roots and grow.

Top Tip

You can skip the pricking-out stage by choosing your original seed container wisely. If you use a modular seed tray and put only one seed in each cell, or sow seeds individually in small pots, you won't need to prick out.

How to Prick Out Seedlings

▶ **Prepare the new home:** Fill your chosen pot or seedling tray with moist compost. Choose trays that are 7.5 cm (3 in) deep or pots that are 6 to 7.5 cm (2 ½ to 3 in) in diameter.

▶ **Moisten:** Make sure the compost in the original pots is damp; water if necessary and allow to drain.

▶ **Select:** Choose only the healthiest and strongest looking seedlings to transplant; the rest can go into your compost heap.

▶ **Loosen:** Carefully loosen the soil from underneath the seedling roots with a pencil or dibber.

▶ **Lift:** Gently lift the seedling from the compost by holding the first set of leaves (the ones closest to the root). Never hold by the second set or the stem.

▶ **Plant:** Use your finger, pencil or dibber to make a small hole in the new compost and put the seedling in its new place. Fill in the hole around the roots and firm down gently.

Hardening Off

If you've grown seedlings indoors and want to move them outdoors – to a garden bed, for example – you'll need to harden them off first. Hardening off means acclimatizing the seedlings to lower temperatures. If you take a seedling grown indoors and plant it straight out into the garden it might get shocked, stop growing or even die. Hardening off seedlings is a gradual process.

Top Tip

You can use a cold frame to make hardening off easier. Simply open the lid on the cold frame a little more each day during the course of a week and close it again at night time

131

How to Harden Off Seedlings

Begin the hardening off process about a week before you want to transplant the seedlings.

▶ **For the first three days:** Place your seedlings, in their pots, in a sheltered spot such as an open porch or on a bench under a tree during the day. Bring them back indoors at night or if the temperature suddenly changes during the day.

▶ **For the next three days:** Increase the amount of time the seedlings are exposed to the elements. Keep them in the sun for half a day and then put them in a sheltered space for the rest of the day before bringing them indoors at night.

▶ **You are now ready to transplant your seedlings:** Choose a day when it is neither too sunny, rainy or windy to do this.

Transplanting Seedlings

It is important to choose the ideal weather conditions for transplanting, and it is crucial to ensure that all risk of frosts has passed. Overcast but warm is ideal, or you can transplant seedlings in the evening when it's cooler. If it is too hot and sunny or windy, the plants will dry out quickly. Work as quickly and carefully as you can with transplanting. The plants may wilt quite a lot when first transplanted, so get them out of the pot and into the soil as quickly as you can.

Top Tip

Keep a written plan
of your garden so
that you don't forget
where you have
planted things!

How to Transplant Seedlings

▶ **Water thoroughly:** The day before transplanting, water both the seedlings and their new outdoor planting places well.

▶ **Remove seedlings from pots:** Turn the pot over while holding the plant stem gently between the forefinger and middle finger of your other hand. You should be able to give the pot a gentle tap and the root system and all the soil will come out in one ball.

▶ **Dig holes for your plants:** The new planting place should be the same depth as the root ball plus allow for about 2.5 cm (1 in) of stem.

▶ **Firm them in:** Once the plants are in their new place, firm the soil gently around them and water.

▶ **Water well:** Over the next few days make sure they get enough water and they will start to pick up.

▶ **Fertilize:** It is a good idea to give the transplanted seedlings a boost with some liquid all-purpose fertilizer.

▶ **Protect from bad weather:** You can pop cloches over the plants to keep them warm and protect them from heavy rainfall if necessary.

133

Plant Care

Make sure you keep plants well watered. The amount of water your plants need will depend on the climate, your soil type and whether your plants are in containers or an open site such as a traditional garden bed. It is better to give established plants a good soak twice a week than water them little and often. If you water them little and often they don't put down deep roots in search for water and they can become weak.

Watering

The best time of day to water your plants is in the evening after the sun has gone down. This means your plants get more of the water and less evaporates. Try to get the water where it is needed; instead of watering all over the plant, direct the water towards the stem of each plant so that it soaks down to the roots. This is easy if you have a few plants in containers, but not as simple if you have a lot of plants to take care of. In some weathers you won't need to water at all; night-time rains coupled with warm sunny days make gardening easy!

Top Tip

Use the finest watering-can rose you can find to water freshly sown seeds otherwise the force of the water will make the seeds float to the top of your soil.

Watering Containers

Be aware that if you are growing in containers, you may need to water them every day, even if there has been rainfall because the leaves can prevent the rain getting to the soil.

Top Tip

You can help prevent weeds growing by putting mulch around your vegetable plants to cover up any bare soil.

Adding Fertilizer

If your soil is rich in nutrients, your crops will grow well, but you might like to use an all-purpose fertilizer too. Whether you choose granules, pellets, liquids, organic or non-organic is up to you. Read the manufacturer's guidelines for advice on how often to use them and on dosages.

Weeding

Weeding is tedious, but essential if you want a good crop from your plants.

Weeds will take nutrients and water from the soil, which means less for your plants. In addition, weeds such as bindweed will wrap themselves around your plants and choke them. If you are growing plants in containers, you can carefully pick out individual weeds by hand. If you are growing in raised beds or garden beds you can hoe them off between your vegetables. With a hoe you just slice the weeds off where they come out of the ground without disturbing the soil surface. If you are not growing organically, you can use weed killers, but you must be very careful not to get them on your vegetables and herbs. Follow manufacturer's recommendations for dosage and use.

Organic Growing

You might prefer to grow organically. Organic gardening is not easy to define but, put simply, organic gardeners do not use harmful synthetic pesticides, herbicides or fertilizers. In addition, they tend to work with nature, rather than against it, attracting beneficial wildlife to their gardens, utilizing companion planting and making their own compost so that any plant 'waste' is turned back into a valuable resource. It is a sustainable method of gardening with benefits to both you and the environment.

Benefits of Organic Gardening

Here are just a few things that benefit from going organic:

▶ **Soil:** Organic growing avoids the use of synthetic chemical sprays, which can upset soil balance and cause soil erosion.

▶ **Money:** Some organic produce is expensive to buy in the shops. By growing your own, you'll save money and be able to eat more organic food.

▶ **Water:** Chemical pesticides, herbicides and fertilizers eventually end up in the water supply, thereby polluting the environment and harming wildlife.

▶ **Environment:** Animals, birds and beneficial insects are not harmed by organic gardening and will be attracted to your garden.

▶ **Health:** Organic vegetables contain more of certain vitamins and minerals, such as vitamin C.

▶ **Taste:** Organic produce generally tastes better than that grown with artificial fertilizers and soil enhancers.

Did You Know?

French Marigolds (*Tagetes petula*) are easy and effective companion plants to grow: plant them anywhere around your crops for a beautiful and beneficial display.

Small Steps Towards Organic

If you find the thought of gardening without the use of powerful pesticides and weedkillers daunting, you could switch to organic gardening gradually. The first year you might make and use your own compost. The second year you could do some companion planting. The third year you could set up a wildlife garden and the fourth investigate some organic ways of dealing with pests and diseases. The number one requirement of any gardening method should be to look after the soil. If you do that, the plants will grow well.

Extending the Season

Our seasons are changing every year. In some areas frosts arrive in the middle of spring while autumn seems to set in before the summer has started! If you are sowing and growing outdoors seeds may not germinate fast enough, seedlings may struggle to grow and cold can set in before your crop has reached maturity. Thankfully, there are some things you can do to extend your growing season.

Tips for Extending the Growing Season

▶ **Warming soil:** After preparing the soil for spring sowing, cover the soil with a thick layer of mulch or black polythene for a few weeks to warm up the soil.

▶ **Indoor sowing:** Sow seeds indoors on a sunny windowsill or in a greenhouse to give them a head start.

▶ **Cold frames:** Use a cold frame to acclimatize plants to cooler temperatures.

▶ **Fleece and cloches:** After transplanting, cover delicate plants with horticultural fleece. If you don't have fleece you can use cloches instead. These are like mini greenhouses that sit over individual plants. Old plastic bottles work too.

▶ **Polytunnels and greenhouses:** You can construct a polytunnel of any size to warm up the soil and keep seedlings protected from cold temperatures and strong winds. Greenhouses are ideal for sowing seeds and crops that love heat, such as tomatoes and peppers.

Checklist

▶ Check seed packets to see **when** you need to start sowing.

▶ Prepare your soil to a **fine tilth** in early spring.

▶ Check to see if your seeds need to be planted in situ or whether they can be **transplanted** later.

▶ Consider the use of **seed tapes or seed mats** if these would be helpful.

▶ Make sure you have enough **seed compost** for your seeds.

▶ Make sure your soil is **warm and dry** enough to begin sowing seeds.

▶ Remember to **water** seedlings frequently as they emerge but water larger plants less frequently.

▶ Gather together any materials you might need to **extend your growing season** such as fleece, cloches or a polytunnel.

▶ Make sure you have **enough pots** for final transplanting if you are container gardening.

Reaping

The

Rewards

Harvesting Your Crop

You're about to reap the rewards of all your hard work! One of the most exciting times in gardening is when your harvest is ready to eat. Often a glut of food will come at once, so learning basic harvesting, storage and preservation methods can help you prevent food waste and enjoy more of your home-grown food.

Planning Your Harvest

With careful planning, you can harvest food all year round, although late summer and early autumn are generally the times when you are most likely to have a glut. If you find yourself with a massive glut of something for a fortnight and then nothing else to eat for several weeks, you've not made the most of your garden.

Some crops can be left in the ground until you need them, whereas others need picking at the peak of ripeness and eating straight away to be fully enjoyed. Some crops store well in a cool, dark place. Others will need different methods of storage such as bottling, drying, freezing or pickling.

Tips for a Successful Harvest

▶ **Thoughtful quantities:** Don't grow too much of any one thing but make sure you grow enough of the crops you love.

▶ **Stagger the harvest:** Choose varieties of the same crop that will mature at different times. Cabbages are a classic example: there is a variety for every season.

▶ **Extend the harvest:** By sowing a few seeds every few days you'll extend your harvest season. Lettuces and radishes are ideal for this.

▶ **Preserve the glut:** If you find yourself with a glut of something, learn how to preserve it to get the maximum from your harvest.

Top Tip

Seed packets will give harvesting times. Try to space your crops out to give you time to make the most of each harvest.

When to Harvest

Seed packets will give guidelines about when to harvest your produce and you'll find further information in chapter eight of this book. Don't just go by the guidelines, however. As your gardening experience grows, you'll get to know the right time for harvesting. Crops will have a look, a smell or a feel that tells you they are perfect for eating and this sense will develop as you grow more produce.

Learning About Ripeness

Learning when a vegetable or herb is ready for eating is an art that you will develop with experience. Some foods are easier than others: potatoes, for example, are generally ready when the flowers die back and the plants keel over; onions are ready when the plant goes brown and wilts. Other crops show more subtle changes that indicate ripeness. A tomato gradually changes colour, but if it turns too red it is past its peak. Runner beans need to be picked before the pods become stringy and tough.

Developing Your Own Taste

Not everyone has the same taste! You might want to pick a courgette while it is young and tender, before it grows into a tasteless marrow. Someone else, whose favourite meal is stuffed marrow, might consider that the bigger a courgette grows the better! Some people eat broad beans only when they are young, small and the pods can be eaten as well. Others are not interested in the pods, only in the beans themselves, so will wait until the beans are larger before picking them. One person loves a green pepper, whereas another will not eat it until it has turned red. Beetroot are delicious when golf-ball sized, but store better if picked larger.

144

Producing Fruit or Seeds?

Some crops need regular picking otherwise they stop growing. The aim of a plant is to create seeds for new plants the following season, not to feed you for several weeks. Your aim, as a gardener, is to harvest the fruits of your labour before the plant stops producing food!

Crops That Need Regular Harvesting

If you don't pick the tender pods of runner beans, for example, they will quickly grow into huge, inedible tough pods with large beans inside, which are next year's seeds. Once this happens, the plant stops producing beans because it has done its job. Marrows and broad beans are the same, but if you pick them frequently, you'll trick the plant into thinking it needs to keep producing more fruit to produce seeds. Beans, peas, tomatoes and courgettes all need regular attention and daily or every-other-day harvesting.

Plants With a Longer Harvesting Season

Fortunately, many other vegetables are less fussy and will give you a long harvesting season. Carrots and potatoes are excellent; they sit in the ground until you are ready to eat them. Leeks, sprouts and kale will stay in the ground until required, needing little care and attention. Winter cabbages and squash will keep growing steadily until you eat them.

Top Tip

If you break a runner bean in half and it snaps cleanly without bending or leaving strings, it is perfectly ripe. If it's stringy, it has gone beyond its best.

Harvesting Tools

If you are growing food in containers, all you need to harvest your crops are your hands, a knife or sharp pair of scissors and perhaps a small hand fork. If you are growing food in raised beds

145

or traditional garden beds you will need a long-handled fork too. If you are harvesting a lot of food at once, you will also need something to carry your produce in. Garden trugs are ideal, but any clean basket or container will do.

How to Harvest

How you harvest each crop will vary depending on whether it is the leaves, the fruit or the roots that are eaten. When harvesting, you need to be gentle to avoid damaging nearby crops or the plant itself.

Harvesting Leaves

If you are growing cut-and-come-again spinach or salads you can pick the leaves by hand, but make sure you hold the plant stem at the base so you don't pull the entire plant out of the soil. Make sure that you leave 2.5–5 cm (1–2 in) of stem to ensure regrowth. You will need a sharp knife for plants such as kale, otherwise you risk tearing the stems, which could prevent further regrowth or leave the plant susceptible to disease or attack. It is

Top Tip

Pinch out the tips of basil plants to encourage bushy plants rather than tall, leggy stems.

better to cut herbs with sharp scissors or pull off individual leaves by hand to prevent uprooting the entire plant.

Harvesting Fruiting Plants

Tomatoes are best harvested with their green calyx attached. You will know when a tomato is ready because it will come away from the vine with little force. Peppers are best cut with a tiny stem and so are courgettes; if you try to pull a courgette away from the plant, you risk damaging the crop. Peas and beans can be harvested by hand, but you will need to steady the plant stem with your other hand to prevent damage or uprooting the plant.

Harvesting Roots

There are different requirements for harvesting root crops than those that grow above ground. To lift potatoes you will need to gently loosen the soil around the plant with a fork and then use your hands to find your treasure. If you use a fork for finding potatoes, you will probably spear one or two casualties with the prongs. Depending on your soil type, you should be able to pull up most other root crops, such as radishes, beetroot and carrots, by hand, though if your soil is heavy you might need to loosen the earth first with a hand fork.

Storing Produce

Vegetables are arguably at their best when picked at their peak of ripeness, then prepared and eaten within minutes of harvesting. Whenever possible, pick only as much food as you will eat right away. At certain times, however, you may get a glut, and then you will need to store or preserve it. You will be able to enjoy more of your garden produce if you learn how best to store your crops and have a go at preserving some of them.

Why Store Produce?

Storing produce is the key to self-sufficiency. It is said that a family of four can be self-sufficient with just an acre of land if they know how to harvest and store food correctly. Unfortunately we see food as a cheap commodity and, if it runs out or we need to throw some away, we simply

Did You Know?

The best time for harvesting is mid-morning, after any dew has disappeared but before the sun gets too hot.

visit the supermarket and buy more. Before our food was transported across the globe, there was no salad in the winter or strawberries in springtime; people simply went without! There is little point growing lovely vegetables and herbs if you don't harvest them at the right time or store them properly to enjoy them throughout the year.

Reasons to Store

If you learn some basic storage and preserving techniques, you will be able to:

▶ **Save money:** By carefully storing your own harvest, you won't need to buy food from the shops.

▶ **Reduce food miles:** Instead of buying tomatoes from Italy, you can preserve your own and reduce your personal food miles.

▶ **Reduce food waste:** With careful food storage there will be little to throw away.

▶ **Reduce food packaging:** You can use reusable packaging instead of disposable plastic bags for your home-grown harvest.

▶ **Eat healthier food:** You know exactly how your food has been grown and whether it has pesticides on it.

▶ **Feel good:** There is great satisfaction to be had in knowing that you have grown, harvested and preserved your own food!

149

Short-term Storage

You might pick three or four days' worth of something and need to store it only temporarily before eating it. Once you have picked something, you need to slow down its rate of deterioration. As soon as a vegetable has been picked from the plant, the sugar begins to turn to starch. In some plants, such as sweetcorn and peas, this happens very quickly. The result is tough, tasteless food. Some vegetables need refrigerating straight away to stop the ripening process. Others, such as tomatoes, should not be put into the fridge because this changes their flavour and texture.

Refrigeration

Many people do not know how to get the most out of their refrigerators and the result can be that food goes off quickly. A refrigerator should be neither too hot nor too cold: the ideal temperature range is 1°– 4°C (34°–39°F). Above this temperature, bacteria can multiply quickly and below it the texture and taste of food can be spoilt. Food needs air to circulate around it, so don't stuff your refrigerator too full.

Ethylene

Some foods emit a chemical called ethylene, which can increase the speed at which produce deteriorates. Ethylene tends to turn broccoli yellow, add a bitterness and floppiness to carrots and cucumber and cause brown spots on leafy crops and beans. Ideally, you should keep foods that emit ethylene away from those that are sensitive to it by using sealed containers.

150

Foods That Emit Ethylene

- Apples
- Avocados
- Bananas
- Melons
- Nectarines

- Pears
- Peaches
- Plums
- Tomatoes

Foods Most Adversely Affected by Ethylene

- Broccoli
- Brussels sprouts
- Cabbage
- Carrots

- Cucumbers
- Peas
- Peppers

Longevity of Produce

Some foods deteriorate more quickly than others. It can be useful to know which vegetables and herbs will last longest so that you can menu plan around the ones that need using up first.

Eat Within a Couple of Days of Harvesting

- Basil
- Broccoli
- Green beans

- Salad leaves
- Watercress
- Sweetcorn

151

Eat Within Five Days of Harvesting

▶ Aubergines
▶ Courgettes
▶ Cucumbers
▶ Lettuce

Eat Within a Week of Harvesting

▶ Brussels sprouts
▶ Cauliflower
▶ Leeks
▶ Mint
▶ Oregano
▶ Parsley
▶ Peppers
▶ Spinach
▶ Tomatoes (although they taste better fresher!)

Vegetables That Can Be Stored Longer Than a Week

▶ Beetroot   ▶ Onions
▶ Cabbage   ▶ Potatoes
▶ Carrots   ▶ Winter squash
▶ Garlic

Top Tip

Wash vegetables before eating, not before refrigerating, to increase lifespan.

152

Short-term Storage Tips

Here are a few tips to help you prolong the life of fresh food in your refrigerator:

▶ **Broccoli:** Store broccoli like cut flowers, with their stems in a glass of water.

▶ **Herbs:** Store herbs with their stems in a glass of water on the work surface or in a cool place.

▶ **Leafy crops:** Spray leafy crops such as spinach with water, shake off the excess and put them in a plastic container with a tight-fitting lid before refrigeration.

▶ **Lettuce:** Pull apart a lettuce and store the separate leaves in a bowl of cold water in the fridge.

▶ **Radishes:** Discard the leaves of radishes and store them in a jar of cold water in the fridge to prevent them going soft.

▶ **In general:** Put a sheet of kitchen towel into the bottom of plastic containers to absorb excess moisture. Moisture can make some produce spoil quickly. Never store less than perfect produce; eat it up right away or turn it into soup.

Long-term Storage

Sometimes you will harvest more produce than you can use in a few days. Some crops – root vegetables and some of the winter vegetables such as cabbages, for example – are easy to store. As long as you have the space, most of these winter crops can be stored in the ground until you need them. Failing that, you can store them in a cool, dark, airy place. Others, however, will need to be harvested and preserved, for example by freezing, bottling, pickling or drying.

The Importance of Good Ventilation

The key to successful long-term storage is ventilation. If crops get too humid they begin to rot. This is why it is not advisable to store food long term in plastic bags. Potatoes store well in hessian, paper or cotton – an old pillowcase is ideal. They need to be kept dark so that they do not go green or begin to sprout. Other root crops, such as carrots, beetroot and parsnips, were traditionally stored in boxes of peat. Peat is no longer an environmentally friendly choice, but you can use sand instead.

Top Tip

Although tomatoes will ripen after they have been picked, they taste better if left to ripen on the vine.

Storing Root Vegetables in Sand

To store root crops in sand, layer the crops between layers of sand like lasagna. Use sand that is only just moist; if it is too wet the crops will rot. Finish with a layer of sand to keep your produce in the dark and store the whole lot in a cool, frost-free place such as a garage. Don't wash the crops before storing, just brush off excess soil and remove the foliage about an inch from the top of the root. Make sure the vegetables are not touching so that air can circulate between them. It goes without saying that you should store only perfect specimens. Anything with signs of pest damage or disease should be eaten up straight away and not stored.

Stringing and Plaiting Onions and Garlic

Who can resist a bunch of onions that have been strung together? While they look lovely, however, they will not last long if you store them in the house; they need to be kept in a cool, dry place until you are ready to use them. There are directions for stringing your own onions available on the Internet. Garden

155

Stew has some good directions with clear photographs to help you www.gardenstew.com/about11490. While over on Bloomingfields Farm site, you will find directions for making garlic plaits, again with helpful photographs www.bloomingfieldsfarm.com/garbrdhow.

Hanging Vegetables

If you don't have enough onions to make a string, the simplest way to store them is to hang them in a dry, cool place. Be aware that a shed can suffer extremes of temperature – freezing in the winter and very hot in the summer. A garage might be better, provided that there are not too many fumes and the area is not damp. Experiment with hanging in different places and see which works best. Pumpkins, marrows and squashes can also be hung. Old nets, such as the ones that some fruit and vegetables come in, are ideal for hanging vegetables. Old laddered tights, too, make a great reuse of materials.

Clamping Root Vegetables

Another traditional method of storing root vegetables is clamping, which is a way of storing them outside on the earth, often in a part of the vegetable patch. They are contained in what is almost like an igloo with a 'chimney' to allow for ventilation.

Top Tip
Fruits such as citrus fruits and onions often come in small net bags. Hold on to these and use them to hang your own produce such as squash.

How to Make a Clamp

▶ **Site:** Select a sheltered, well-drained site on your soil. If your soil becomes waterlogged in the winter, you won't be able to use a clamp.

▶ **Layers:** Line the base of your chosen area with straw and put a layer of soil on to the bed of straw.

▶ **Veg:** Place healthy, dry root vegetables on to the soil in a mound. Once you have stacked up your vegetables, cover with a thick layer of straw.

▶ **Earth:** Scrape earth from around the vegetables and build it up around the mound of vegetables and straw, like a sand castle. Use earth up to a depth of 15 cm (6 in). Make sure the clamp has steep sides to allow rainwater to run off.

▶ **Ventilation:** Stick a few pieces of straw upright into the mound to act as 'chimneys' – these allow moisture and heat to escape.

▶ **Use:** When you need some vegetables, take them out of the clamp and rebuild the clamp to protect the rest of the crop.

Bottling

Bottling is simple to do and can be done on the hob or in the oven. You don't need any special equipment, just some kilner jars, a stack of tea towels and a decent pair of oven gloves. (Bottling is also referred to as canning, which can cause some confusion. In fact, 'canning' has nothing to do with the use of cans.) When you bottle foods, you preserve them in airtight glass jars. The foods are heated to a high temperature to prevent bacteria, yeasts and mould growing and as the jars cool, a seal forms, which makes the contents air tight.

What to Bottle

It is more usual to bottle fruits than vegetables, because fruits are higher in acid, which prevents the growth of bacteria. Tomatoes, with their naturally high acid content, can be successfully and safely bottled at home. You can then use your bottled tomatoes for soups, stews or pasta sauces throughout the year. Due to their low acid content, it is better to choose other preservation methods for the vegetables that you grow at home.

How to Bottle Tomatoes

The simplest way to bottle tomatoes is in the oven.

▶ **Remove the skins:** The easiest way is to pour boiling water over a bowl of tomatoes, let them sit for one minute then drain. Once they are cooled you will be able to slip off the skins easily.

▶ **Sterilize:** While you are removing the tomato skins, sterilize the jars and lids you are going to use.

▶ **Turn oven on:** Preheat the oven to 150°C (300°F).

▶ **Blend:** If you want to make passata, put the tomatoes in a blender and then sieve to remove the pips before putting into glass jars.

▶ **Fill jars:** Fill each jar with chopped, skinned tomatoes. Add some salt and a squeeze of lemon juice to each jar.

Top Tip

Ask your friends and family to save old jam jars for you throughout the year; these are ideal for making your own pickles and chutneys.

▶ **Heat:** Put the jars on a baking sheet, leaving room between each jar, and place in the preheated oven for 11/2 hours.

▶ **Seal:** Take out the jars carefully and, wrapping your hands in tea towels and/or oven gloves, get the lids on the jars as quickly as you can. As the jars cool, they will form a vacuum and become air tight. Discard any jars that have not formed a seal after a couple of hours.

▶ **Store:** Label, date and store the jars in a cool, dark place.

159

Drying

Drying is an old method of preserving food that removes moisture that causes food to rot. Suitable vegetables for drying include tomatoes, mushrooms and courgettes, but feel free to experiment with anything. Drying is also perfect for herbs. The traditional way of drying is to sun dry, but indoor air drying and drying in an oven or an electric dehydrator are now more common. Once you have dried your vegetables and herbs, keep them in an airtight container to prevent them absorbing moisture from the air.

Air Drying Herbs

Air drying is particularly suitable for herbs. The best time to harvest herbs for air drying is just before the flower buds appear, as this is when the leaves contain the most oil and therefore the most taste.

▶ **Collect:** Cut the stems mid-morning, after any dew has dried and before it gets too hot. Choose only perfect leaves for drying. Shake the stems to remove insects or debris.

▶ **Bundle:** Select five stems and tie them together with string. If you dry too many at once they might go mouldy.

▶ **Hang:** Hang them upside down in a room that is airy but does not get direct sunlight. You will need to leave the herbs to dry for between one and two weeks.

Storing Dried Herbs

Once the herbs are dry, check that none have gone mouldy, then remove the leaves from the stems by rubbing your hand along the length of the stem.

You can gently crush the leaves if you wish, but better flavour is preserved in the whole leaves. Put the dried leaves in an airtight container, label and date them and store in a dark, dry place away from sunlight. After a couple of days, check to make sure there is no moisture inside the container. If there is, take the leaves out and dry them for longer. Herbs will store for years, but are best used within a year for fuller flavour. The exception is sage, which becomes stronger in taste over time.

Drying Herbs for Seeds

To gather the seeds of herbs such as fennel or coriander, harvest the stems before the seed heads turn brown. (If they turn brown, you will probably lose most of the seeds when you cut the plant!) Cut the entire head off the plant and place it in a clean, dry paper bag. Place the bags in a warm, dry area, such as an airing cupboard, but ensure that there is good ventilation around the bag and seed head. Seed heads may take as long as six weeks to dry, so be patient. After that time, shake the seeds loose into the bag, remove any debris and store the seeds in airtight containers.

Air Drying Peas and Beans

Although most vegetables are best dried in an oven or with an electric dehydrator, peas and beans can be air dried. The procedure is simple as most of the drying can take place on the plant after you have harvested the ones you want to eat fresh. If the weather gets very wet, you will need to remove the plants and bring them indoors. Hang the crop up (it is easier if you leave the pods attached to the stems) until completely dry, when the pods will be brittle and break easily. Remove the beans and peas from their pods and lay them on a piece of muslin stretched between two pieces of wood. Continue drying for a week until completely dried. Place in airtight containers, label, date and store. Dried peas and beans are superb ingredients for soups and stews.

Top Tip

Why not have a go at air drying other vegetables too? Slice them thinly and place on muslin sheets, then place in an airing cupboard with the door slightly ajar to allow good ventilation.

Oven Drying Vegetables

Drying vegetables in an oven is ideal if you do not have a dehydrator. The aim of dehydrating is not to cook the vegetables, but to draw out as much moisture as you can to prevent food spoiling. As with all preserving methods, select only the best vegetables to dry. Dried vegetables should last about 6-12 months.

How to Oven Dry Vegetables

▶ **Preheat:** Set your oven to its lowest setting (around 110°C/225°F/Gas Mark ¼).

▶ **Blanch:** Cut the vegetables into thin slices and blanch (plunge into boiling water and bring back to the boil quickly) for a couple of minutes before draining, plunging them into ice cold water, draining again and blotting dry with clean tea towels.

Top Tip

Don't try to dry vegetables on baking trays or other solid trays because you need as much air as possible to circulate around the food in order to complete the drying process.

▶ **Place on racks:** Cover cooling racks with muslin and carefully space the vegetables on them in a single layer.

▶ **Oven dry:** Put your vegetables in the oven and leave them until they have a leathery texture. You may need to prop open your oven to let moisture escape.

▶ **Monitor:** Dehydrating can take from a few hours to 24 hours. Be patient, keep checking and record your experiences. Don't be tempted to turn up the oven temperature or you run the risk of cooking the vegetables.

163

▶ **Cool and store:** Once they are ready, leave them to cool completely before putting in airtight containers. Label, date and store in a cool, dark place.

Using a Dehydrator

Dehydrators work in the same way as an oven but are more convenient to use. You can get more in them because they use stacking trays and you can't accidentally cook vegetables in them. A dehydrator will take around 8–12 hours to dry vegetables depending on the size you have cut them and the amount of moisture in the food. Prepare vegetables as above – cut into uniform pieces and blanch for a couple of minutes. Place the vegetables on the dehydrator trays and follow the manufacturer's guidelines for approximate times. Once dried, cool completely before storing in airtight containers. Label, date and store in a cool, dark place.

Freezing

One of the most common methods of food preservation is freezing. It's quick, convenient and simple, though freezers cost money to run and you need space for a good-sized one if you have a big harvest. Freezing alters the structure of food, so you can't freeze vegetables and use them raw after defrosting; you should only freeze vegetables and herbs that you want to use in cooked dishes. Blanching vegetables before freezing helps to retain nutrients, colour and structure, so don't be tempted to skip this important step.

Freezing Herbs

You can freeze herbs in ice cube trays and add them at the last minute to your cooking. Remember that you won't be able to defrost herbs and eat them raw; they will have to be cooked. Select herbs just before they flower, when their oils are strongest; this will usually be midsummer. Choose herbs that are in good condition and discard any that have pest damage or disease. Finely chop the herbs and place a tablespoon of each into each compartment of the ice cube tray. Top up with water and freeze. There is no need to defrost them before use; simply add to your dish and warm through. Frozen herbs are ideal for soups, stews, casseroles and pasta sauces.

165

Freezing Vegetables

You will need to do a small amount of preparation before freezing vegetables. Top and tail beans, pod peas and broad beans and chop broccoli, spinach and carrots. Blanch the vegetables then plunge them into ice cold water to stop the cooking process. Drain well, dry and place in freezer-proof containers. Label, date and freeze as soon as the vegetables are cool. Vegetables with high water content, such as courgettes, tomatoes or cucumbers, do not freeze well and will collapse when you cook them. You can freeze them and then make them into sauces and soups, but it's better to make the finished product and freeze that instead.

Vegetables That Freeze Well

▶ Runner and dwarf beans
▶ Peas
▶ Broccoli

▶ Broad beans
▶ Spinach
▶ Carrots

Using Frozen Vegetables

Cook all frozen vegetables straight from the freezer; do not defrost them first. Small vegetables such as peas and finely sliced beans will need only a few minutes' cooking time. Larger vegetables such as carrots and broccoli will need about 12 minutes to cook. Spinach can be added at the end of the cooking time as it doesn't take long to cook through. Sometimes it is better to make the finished dish first and freeze that. This is particularly true of recipes with a lot of tomatoes or courgettes in them such as ratatouille or pasta sauce. Simply batch cook your favourite recipe, allow to cool, store in freezer-proof containers, label, date and put into the freezer. Heat through from frozen and make sure the meal is thoroughly warmed through before serving.

Top Tip

Some vegetables freeze together in clumps. Avoid this by freezing blanched produce on trays. Once it's frozen, put it into bags or containers.

Pickling

Pickling is another popular method of preserving and most people have a favourite chutney or pickle recipe passed down to them through their family. Different world cuisines define chutneys, pickles and relishes in different ways, but in this book we will assume that pickles and chutneys are ingredients preserved in sugar, vinegar and spices, which are sealed in glass jars.

Types of Pickle

Pickles and chutneys use natural preservatives such as vinegar and sugar to preserve food. Easy chutneys to make, and those that are useful for using up a glut of vegetables, include green tomato and marrow. Another handy recipe to have is runner bean chutney. Common pickled vegetables include onions and beetroot. Piccalilli is another favourite pickle. It is made from cauliflower and other vegetables and coloured with turmeric.

Did You Know?

Iron or copper pans can react with acid in the vinegar. Always use a stainless-steel pan for making chutney.

Chutney

Chutney is a wonderful thing to make because the possibilities are endless. Measurements don't have to be precise and if you

167

don't have one of the ingredients, you can substitute with another (though you must use the vinegar and sugar!). Ordinary malt vinegar will do for chutney, but you can use cider vinegar if you prefer. You will find specific recipes on the Internet or in cookery books, but the best ones are often obtained via word of mouth!

How to Make Chutney

▶ **Prepare:** Cut ingredients into even-sized small chunks. (Use only perfect specimens.) Place your ingredients in a large stainless-steel pan.

▶ **Cook:** Add vinegar, sugar and spices. Gradually bring to the boil, stirring all the time to dissolve the sugar. Simmer the mixture until it is syrupy and no liquid leaches out. Depending on the quantities you are cooking, this can take anything from one hour to several hours.

▶ **Sterilize:** While the chutney is cooking, sterilize your jars. Use either old jam jars that have a plastic coating inside the lids or kilner jars. (Lids with metal inners can react with the vinegar.) To sterilize your jars, wash them thoroughly, along with their lids, and place them in the oven at 100°C (210°F) for 15 minutes.

▶ **Fill:** Carefully remove the jars from the oven and spoon the hot chutney into the hot jars. Seal and leave to cool.

▶ **Label and store:** Once the chutney has cooled down and the lids have formed a seal you can date and label the jars. Keep chutney for three months before eating to allow the vinegar to mellow and the flavours to infuse. Once opened, keep the chutney refrigerated and use within one month.

Checklist

▶ Think about which of the **various methods** of preservation – bottling, drying, freezing and pickling – might suit you and the crops you plan to grow.

▶ Think of your **reasons for storing** your produce: whether it is to save money, lower your impact on the environment or for health reasons.

▶ **Plan your harvest** carefully: could you prevent a glut by successive sowing or by choosing varieties that mature at different times of the year?

▶ Don't store crops that produce **ethylene** next to those that are susceptible to its effects.

▶ If you have the room, try **clamping** as an effective and simple way to store root crops.

▶ Collect suitable **jars** for bottling tomatoes and for making pickles and chutneys.

▶ Air dry and/or freeze **herbs.**

▶ Experiment with **dehydrating** different varieties of vegetables in the oven, remembering to make a note of your results, with times.

▶ Try some new **pickle and chutney recipes** – a great way to use up a glut of vegetables!

Pests And Problems

Pests

There is nothing as soul destroying as seeing your crops attacked by pests. Unfortunately, pests are a part of every gardener's life, no matter how experienced they are. There are, however, many ways to prevent pests, as well as to deal with them. If you know what you're looking for and how to treat your plants, you stand a better chance of saving them.

Prevention is Better Than Cure

The saying is certainly true in the garden. With careful management you can prevent most pests attacking your produce, and with vigilant observation you can prevent too much damage if you do get any. Damage may be small and insignificant, such as a couple of tiny holes in a leaf, or it can be major, such as the destruction of a crop.

Prevention Tips

There are many ways to prevent pests attacking your crops. Here are some of them.

▶ **Beneficial wildlife:** By attracting natural predators to your garden you can reduce pest damage.

▶ **Natural sprays:** You can repel pests with natural sprays made from plant extracts.

172

▶ **Companion planting:** This helps confuse pests by covering up the scent of the plants they are attracted to.

▶ **Plants that repel:** Some plants, especially herbs, repel pests with their strong oils.

▶ **Barriers, deterrents and traps:** Deter pests by using barriers, deterrents and traps such as fencing for mammals, CDs for scaring birds and beer traps for slugs.

▶ **Healthy soil:** This leads to healthy plants, which are less susceptible to attack.

▶ **Sowing times:** Sowing at the right time can decrease pest damage.

▶ **Tidy spaces:** Keeping your garden tidy means pests will have fewer places to hide.

▶ **Rotation:** Crop rotation reduces the risk of pests building up in the soil.

▶ **Spacing:** Overcrowding can lead to pest problems. Give each plant enough room to get the nutrients, water and sunlight it needs.

▶ **Regular checks:** Make checking your plants for signs of pest attack a regular part of maintenance. It is easy to rub off a few aphids with your finger; treating an infestation is more difficult.

▶ **Biological control:** If you can't attract enough beneficial insects to your garden, you can import natural predators and parasites.

Pesticides

Some gardeners use pesticides but, while these are quick and effective for getting rid of pests, some of the side effects are not so impressive. Short term, pesticides can be hazardous to children and pets if they come in contact with the crops you have treated or the chemicals themselves. In the long term, synthetic pesticides are harmful to the environment. Eventually they pollute the soil, air and water. In addition, pesticides can wipe out beneficial insects and predators in your garden, which puts you back at the beginning – lacking in natural defences for a healthy garden.

'Natural' Pesticides

If you do need to take corrective action, a range of more environmentally friendly products are available. Even though they might be approved for organic gardening, they may still kill beneficial insects, however, so think carefully before using them.

Reducing the Negative Effects of Pesticides

Here are some tips for reducing environmental damage when using natural or synthetic pesticides.

- ▶ Always follow the manufacturer's instructions.
- ▶ Use pesticides for treatment, not as a preventative.
- ▶ Only make up as much as you need.
- ▶ Never store made-up spray.
- ▶ Choose a still day without a breeze to prevent drift.
- ▶ Spray in the evening when bees are not working.

Types of Pest

There are many pests that can attack plants in your garden; so many that whole books have been written about them! This book is for people who are new to gardening and deals with the most common ones. You'll find information about the pests, where you might find them, which plants they attack and details about natural predators along with other biological controls and tips for minimizing damage to your crops.

Flies

This section will deal with the most common bothersome flies: whitefly, aphids (also known as blackfly or greenfly) and carrot fly. Treatment is similar for each and includes attracting natural predators to your garden and not overcrowding your plants. Covering crops with horticultural fleece is helpful too.

Whitefly

Whiteflies look like tiny white moths. They hide on the underside of leaves and can multiply rapidly, which is why frequent checking of plants should be part of your regular garden maintenance. Whiteflies

> ### Top Tip
> Plant lavender to protect nearby plants from whitefly. It will also attract bees and other beneficial insects to your garden.

reproduce rapidly in hot weather and can become a big problem in greenhouses, although they will attack outdoor crops such as cabbages and Brussels sprouts as well. Whiteflies are attracted to yellow sticky traps, so place them around your garden and over the doors of your greenhouse. Natural predators are lacewings and ladybirds. Biological controls include Encarsia formosa, which is a small wasp, and Delphastus pusillus, a small ladybird beetle. Both of these controls work best at temperatures above 18°C (64°F). You can buy whitefly killer that is based on plant extracts.

Aphids

Also known as greenfly or blackfly, aphids are one of the most common garden pests. They suck the sap from young shoots and will often be found on runner beans, where they leave a sticky residue. The best way to deal with them is to encourage plenty of beneficial insects to your garden; the gardener's favourite is ladybirds. One of the easiest ways to attract ladybirds is with a clump of stinging nettles, where they will lay their eggs. Ladybirds and lacewings will be attracted by calendula and the poached egg plant (Limnanthes douglasii) too. You can also put up bug houses in your garden to encourage beneficial insects to stay. Aphids can be washed off leaves with a jet of water or nettle tea, but make sure you don't damage the plant.

Carrot Fly

It is the maggots of carrot fly that burrow into carrots and parsnips. They can kill young carrots or make carrots inedible due to tunnelling. Female carrot flies are attracted to the smell released from carrot leaves, so the secret is to treat carrots gently. When you thin out or pull up a mature carrot, be careful not to bruise the leaves of nearby carrots as this releases the smell. You can disguise the smell of carrot leaves by planting onions or sage nearby. Carrot flies cannot fly higher than two feet, so you can build high barriers around carrot beds or plant them in containers off the ground. Cover large areas of carrots with horticultural fleece.

Caterpillars, Moths and Butterflies

Did You Know?

Basil is a great plant for the garden – it repels all kinds of flies, including aphids, and attracts bees.

Butterflies are beautiful to look at, but they lay eggs that can cause problems when you're trying to grow food to eat. Nearly everybody can recognize the Cabbage White butterfly (Pieris brassicae), which can be seen flitting around the garden on warm, sunny days. The Pea Moth (*Cydia nigricana*) is another common pest, which will eat your peas before you do. Covering crops is a good deterrent and you can pick caterpillars off by hand.

Pea Moth

Pea Moth caterpillars are white with black dots and feed on the peas inside the pods. You don't always know you have them until the peas are podded, when you will find the Pea Moths have got to your peas before you. Eggs are laid between June and August. You can either use horticultural fleece between June and August to prevent eggs being laid on the plants or organize your sowing times so that the pods are not developing at the crucial time. Planting marigolds among your pea crop can repel Pea Moths.

Cabbage White

Cabbage White will munch their way through tough cabbages and leave you with huge holes, which may reach through to the heart of the cabbage. Vigilance is the key: inspect developing cabbages regularly and pick off any caterpillars before they have a chance to cause damage. You can cover cabbages with horticultural fleece to prevent butterflies laying their eggs. Biological control includes the nematode *Steinernema carpocapsae*, which is available from garden centres. Follow the manufacturer's directions for use.

Slugs and Snails

Every gardener's nightmare, slugs and snails can destroy your crops overnight, when they are active (you will see their slimy trails if you have these pests in your garden). Young seedlings are particularly vulnerable whereas established plants are less at risk. The numerous methods used by gardeners to deal with them include putting crushed eggshells or gravel around seedlings, going out at night with a torch and picking slugs and snails off the garden, and using beer traps, copper tapes or neem oil. Neem oil is a powerful insecticide that is safe to use around humans and pets. Rather than actually kill slugs, it interferes with their breeding and eating habits, which means you get fewer slugs next year. Another idea is to make barriers from old plastic bottles, which slugs won't bother to cross.

Birds

Birds come down during the day to peck at crops so are quite easy to scare off, but they can be real pests in some areas. You want to attract birds into your garden to feed off pests, but some birds, such as pigeons, will rob you of your crop too. Pigeons are particularly attracted to cabbages and broccoli, while sparrows will eat the flowers from your runner beans. The best way to keep birds off your crops is to deter them. Either hang shiny, reflective materials, such as old CDs, around the crops you want to protect or cover the plants with horticultural fleece or bird netting.

178

Mammals

Rabbits, mice, badgers and cats, along with other animals, can cause problems in some gardens and can cause a lot of damage by eating peas, beans, sweetcorn and leafy crops. In all cases, deterring the animal is the best way to reduce crop damage.

Small Animals

The best way to deter small animals, such as mice, is to avoid creating cosy areas for them: don't leave garden litter where they might nest! Mice don't like to be disturbed, so make sure you go into your garden every day.

Rabbits and Badgers

If larger mammals such as rabbits or badgers are a problem, the only solution is to make your garden difficult to get into. You'll need strong fencing such as a walk-in cage. Garlic and chilli spray is also said to deter rabbits.

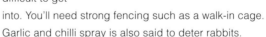

Top Tip

Make your own spray from infused garlic with a squirt of washing-up liquid. Use it to discourage aphids, caterpillars and even rabbits.

Cats

Cats may dig up your seeds when they use your tilthy soil as a handy toilet. You can deter cats with repellent sprays made from cayenne. Covering seeds with fine netting will prevent cats scratching your soil.

179

Disease

It is devastating when your crops are affected by disease. Some diseases cause minor damage, but others can completely destroy your crop. Some diseases, such as blight, are airborne and weather dependent; others, such as blossom end rot, can be caused by bad management in the garden. This section covers some of the more common plant diseases.

Blight

Blight is a fungal disease that mainly affects tomatoes and potatoes. It occurs in warm, wet climates and can wipe out your entire crop. You'll notice a browning of the leaves, which rapidly moves down the stem and can rot the fruit. It moves quickly, so you need to treat it as soon as possible. If you spot the disease on potatoes, remove the above-ground growth and burn it; you may be lucky and prevent it spreading to the tubers. You can arrest blight with infusions of horsetail; a natural anti-fungal treatment. As a preventative for the following year, ensure all potatoes are taken out of the ground at the end of the season. Copper sprays or mancozeb can be bought from garden centres.

Blossom End Rot

Aubergines, tomatoes and peppers can become affected by blossom end rot, which appears as a brown or black bruise shaped in a ring at the base of the fruit. It is easy to prevent because it is a calcium deficiency, usually caused by irregular watering. You should not allow the container you have the plant in to dry out, especially when the plant is flowering and setting fruit. Another cause of blossom end rot is adding fertilizer to soil that is too dry. Only ever add fertilizer to moist soil. You can add mulch around plants to help prevent the soil becoming too dry.

Club Root

Club root is a serious fungal infection that affects brassicas, in particular cabbages, cauliflowers and swedes. Its effects can be seen in swollen, distorted and retarded growth. Club root thrives in wet, acid conditions, so make sure your soil drains well, buy disease-resistant plants or seeds and check the pH of your soil. Liming the soil to make it less acid can help prevent club root. Unfortunately, there is no known cure for club root and affected plants will need to be removed and destroyed. You should also avoid planting brassicas in the same place for several years as the spores can remain dormant in the soil.

Damping Off

As mentioned earlier, damping off can affect any type of seedling, causing the stems to collapse and the plant to die. Prevention is the key, as damping off is the result of overcrowding, over-watering or poor hygiene. Make sure you sterilize all tools and containers before sowing seeds and use fresh seed compost. Do not over-water seedlings; you might find a plant mister more appropriate until the seedling has been potted on. Thin seedlings out as soon as they have two sets of leaves

181

and keep the area well ventilated. Damping off is rarely a problem outdoors because of better airflow and evaporation rates. You can buy a copper fungicide from a garden centre to treat damping off.

Downy Mildew

Downy mildew affects brassicas, lettuce, onions and spinach. Yellow blotches appear on the top of the leaf and grey fungus appears on the underside. Downy mildew can increase in mild, damp and humid weather. You will need to remove and burn diseased crops to prevent it spreading. You can help reduce the risk of infection by leaving adequate space between plants and removing weeds from between them and can treat it with potassium bicarbonate from garden centres. Downy mildew spores can stay in the soil, so good crop rotation is important.

Did You Know?
Borage is a great plant for the garden; it attracts bees, deters cabbage worms, improves the growth of tomatoes and the flowers are edible!

Powdery Mildew

Powdery mildew is a whitish powder that covers leaves and the tips of shoots and can result in stunted or distorted growth. Beetroot, spinach and parsnip leaves are most often affected. It is important to keep plants well watered; mulching around them can help prevent water loss through evaporation, but you should not over-water. Allow good air circulation around plants and pull out weeds, because they can spread powdery mildew. Remove the affected plants and burn them to help prevent it spreading. You can buy anti-fungal preparations made from sulphur from garden centres.

Weeds

Young plants, in particular, need vigilant weeding so that they can receive all the water and nutrients they need from the soil. They also need full access to light for healthy growth. Preparing your bed before sowing and using mulches can reduce the amount of weeding you need to do.

One Man's Weed…

A weed is defined simply as a plant in the wrong place. Some gardeners deliberately plant so-called 'weeds' as wildflowers. For example, some would class St John's wort as a weed, whereas a herbalist would harvest it as a crop. Nettles are usually classed as weeds, but they can be used to make soup in the spring. Some gardeners try to get rid of red clover, but bee lovers welcome it, because of the bees it attracts. Horsetail is a menace when it grows in the wrong place, but it also has some amazing anti-fungal properties. It is worth investigating any positive attributes of your 'weeds' before you decide to rip them all out!

Good Preparation

You can save yourself a lot of work by preparing your plot well before sowing vegetable and herb seeds. Try to get the roots of perennial weeds out when preparing a new area for planting. If you do decide to use a chemical herbicide such as glyphosate, follow the manufacturer's guidelines for use carefully. A more environmentally friendly approach to managing weeds is to cover the ground with a thick layer of mulch.

Weeding Tips

Weeding is a necessary job and one that most gardeners dislike. However, good weeding can increase your harvest and give you a lot of satisfaction! Here are some tips to make weeding easier:

▶ **Keep short accounts:** Try to do a bit of weeding every day. If you pull up weeds while they are young and small it will be much easier and you'll prevent weeds going to seed.

▶ **Use the right tools:** If you are using a hoe, keep it sharp. If you're using a hand fork, invest in a good-quality one that doesn't bend or warp.

▶ **Dig out roots:** If you can get to the roots of perennial weeds, then pull them all out. If you don't, you'll just get more weeds next year.

▶ **Mulch:** Using mulches can help suppress weed growth; use them freely on bare soil.

▶ **Work with the weather:** It is much easier to weed after a light rain shower.

▶ **Don't dig:** Weed seeds can lie dormant in the soil and if you bring them to the surface they will germinate.

184

Weed Types

Just like pests and diseases, there are enough weeds to fill an entire book. This section will tell you more about some of the most common ones and give advice on how to deal with them. There are two main types of garden weed, annual and perennial, each with its own set of characteristics. It is important that you eradicate both types.

Annual Weeds

Annual weeds are less difficult to get rid of than perennial weeds, but they can spread quickly. Annual weeds grow from seeds in the soil, flower and then drop new seeds back into the soil. They can do this very quickly, sometimes several times in one season, which means a patch of weeds can spread over a large surface area very quickly. Commonly found annual weeds include meadow grass, chickweed and shepherd's purse.

Getting Rid of Annual Weeds

Annual weeds respond well to hoeing and hand pulling, but you must get them out before the flowers develop, as these contain the seeds for new weeds. It will be a race

between you and the weeds because they can set seeds very quickly. Annual weed seeds can remain dormant in the soil for years, just waiting for you to dig the soil and bring them to the surface. This is why you can find your bare soil covered with weeds shortly after you have thoroughly dug your plot. It is worth getting hold of a book with clear colour photographs of weeds so that you can learn to recognize them and can pull them out while they are still tiny.

Did You Know?

You might be growing more food in your garden than you realized: 'weeds' such as nettles, ground elder, dandelions and chickweed are edible.

Mulching

Mulches help suppress annual weeds. If you have an infested patch, you might need to be patient and committed for a year. Cover the soil with old carpet held down by bricks. Every month, remove the carpet and pull up any weeds. After a year, you can remove the carpet and prepare the bed. You can also use mulches around your crop to suppress weed growth. Alternatively, use groundcover plants to the same purpose.

Perennial Weeds

Perennial weeds have long roots that can rapidly cover large areas of your garden. The tiniest bit of root left in the soil can produce new weeds. Perennial weeds are difficult to eradicate as many of them have very deep roots, which makes it virtually impossible to pull them all up.

In addition, if you dig too deeply, you risk bringing dormant annual weed seeds up to the surface where they will germinate. This is why many gardeners advocate the 'no-dig' method of gardening. Examples of perennial weeds include stinging nettle, dock, creeping thistle, dandelion, bindweed, horsetail, couch grass and ground elder.

Understanding Perennial Weeds

Perennial weeds are more difficult to get rid of than annual weeds because of their root structure. They can store food in their roots and their leaves take food back into the roots in a cycle. This means they come back year after year. As the leaves replenish the stores in the roots of perennial weeds, it is important to be methodical in your eradication. If you pull up the weeds before the leaves mature

187

you can stop the root stores being replenished with food. If you continue for long enough, eventually the weed will weaken because it will become depleted.

Getting Rid of Perennial Weeds

Perennial weeds spread far-reaching roots under the surface of the soil and are difficult to dig out completely, especially if they have been there for several years. A gardener with an infestation of perennial weeds is often one who will resort to using weedkillers. A product containing glyphosate is the one to go for, but be sure to follow the manufacturer's guidelines for use carefully. However, some weeds, such as horsetail, will not be eradicated, even with the use of strong weedkillers.

Rotovators and Flame Guns

If you are growing organically, you should not use toxic herbicides. There are, however, two other tools that can help you in your battle against weeds: rotovators and flame guns. Rotovators are suitable for annual weeds but should never be used on ground with perennial weeds, as they will simply chop the roots into tiny pieces and each one will then form a new weed. Flame guns can be useful for dealing with small areas of weeds, but must never be used near crops as you risk damaging them as well. Organic gardeners are divided about the use of flame guns because they can also kill beneficial insects as well as the organic matter in the soil.

Checklist

▶ Prevent pests by attracting **beneficial wildlife** into your garden, such as ladybirds.

▶ Use sprays made from **plant extracts** (such as garlic) to repel pests.

▶ Consider **companion planting**, which can confuse pests and throw them off the scent of plants they like.

▶ Keep soil healthy by **rotating crops.**

▶ **Avoid overcrowding** plants; giving them more space can reduce the risk of pest attack.

▶ Reduce the risk of plant diseases by having a **good garden maintenance** regime: regular watering and weeding can help, as can sterilizing any equipment.

▶ If you spot a diseased plant, **work quickly** to solve the issue and prevent the problem spreading.

▶ **Weed** on a daily basis, even if it's just for ten minutes.

▶ Use thick layers of **mulch** to suppress weed growth.

▶ Never rotovate ground that is **contaminated** with perennial weeds.

▶ Pull up annual weeds by hand **before they flower** and drop more seeds.

▶ Some **'weeds' are beneficial**; nettles attract ladybirds into the garden and make a great ingredient for soup!

189

The
Vegetables

A Helpful Directory

You have now learned all the basics for successful gardening – how to prepare the ground, deal with pests, and the best crops for different-sized gardens. This guide will take you through the different crops, giving you tips for the best varieties and how to grow them. The directory is divided into basic plant groups.

A Note on Classification

Classifying vegetable plants into groups can be tricky. For every person who says one thing, there is somebody else who will say another. For example, a swede belongs to the *Cruciferae* family (cabbages, broccoli), but most gardeners class it as a root vegetable. Carrots belong to the *Umbelliferae* family, but they too are normally considered as root crops. Parsley, too, belongs to the *Umbelliferae* family, but it is grown as a herb! Don't get too hung up on what is 'right' or 'wrong'; just find the vegetable you are looking for within this chapter (use the index if necessary) and you'll find all the information you need to help you get started.

Cabbage Family

For the purpose of this book, the cabbage family (sometimes referred to as the *Cruciferae* family or brassicas) includes broccoli, Brussels sprouts, cabbages and kale. Cauliflower has not been included here because, although delicious to eat, they are rather difficult for a beginner to grow. Growing requirements for each are similar, as are the pests and diseases to which they are susceptible. Most members of the cabbage family, including Brussels sprouts, winter cabbages and kale, can stay in the ground throughout the winter to give you an ongoing supply of food. The cabbage family likes slightly alkaline soil, so you may need to add lime before sowing and planting.

Broccoli

Broccoli likes nitrogen-rich soil and full sun. Make sure the soil has plenty of organic matter dug into it when you prepare the bed. You may like to add some nitrogen-rich fertilizer to the soil a couple of weeks before sowing too. An ideal place to plant broccoli is in a bed where there were legumes the previous season because legumes help fix nitrogen into the soil. The tight green or bluish heads of broccoli that are regularly available in supermarkets are also sometimes referred to as calabrese. The other form of broccoli, sprouting broccoli, has either purple or white looser heads. For this section, we will use the terms 'broccoli' and 'sprouting broccoli' to differentiate between them.

193

Growing

▶ **Sowing:** You can sow broccoli in situ as soon as the ground is warm enough. Sow in damp drills and thin out when seedlings appear. Leave broccoli plenty of space to develop a large head and ensure adequate airflow between plants to reduce the risk of disease. Sprouting broccoli can be sown indoors and transplanted later in the year ready for a spring crop. Water the ground before transplanting and firm the plants in well. Sprouting broccoli is hardier and can tolerate heavier soils, so it is the better variety to begin with.

Did You Know?

Broccoli contains as much calcium as milk.

▶ **Varieties:** 'Claret' sprouting broccoli grows well, even on poorer soils, while 'Marathon' is good for compact green heads.

▶ **Tending:** Broccoli requires quite a lot of attention. You need to keep weeds out of the way and the plants watered in dry weather. If the site is exposed, broccoli stalks may need staking to prevent damage. You can mulch around plants to prevent water loss. Feed plants every three to four weeks with nitrogen-rich fertilizer.

▶ **Container gardening:** You may manage to get a few small spears if you have a large enough pot.

Protecting

▶ **Pests:** Birds such as pigeons may eat young broccoli heads, so cover the plants with netting. Caterpillars may damage crops too; pick them off by hand whenever you see them. (It may be advisable to wear gloves with the hairy caterpillars.)

▶ **Diseases:** Plants can be susceptible to club root; if this occurs you will need to dig up the crop and destroy it.

Harvesting and Storing

▶ **Harvesting:** Broccoli can provide a harvest from midsummer through to autumn and again in late winter through to the spring. Harvest broccoli when the heads have developed firm green florets or loose, coloured buds. Regular picking will keep the crop growing for several weeks; cut off the side shoots with a sharp knife as and when you want them.

▶ **Storage:** Both types of broccoli can be stored with their stems in a glass of water in the refrigerator for up to a week and can be successfully frozen.

Eating

Broccoli is best cut into florets and steamed until tender. If you cut it finely, it is good in stir-fries but it can be eaten raw too. Broccoli soup is good when blitzed with soft creamy garlic cheese, or try broccoli and stilton soup for a decadent treat. Broccoli is great in quiches, as a substitute for cauliflower in cauliflower cheese, and goes well with cream in a pasta sauce. You can roast broccoli: toss it in oil with some herbs and bake in the oven until it goes crispy.

Brussels Sprouts

Brussels sprouts are ideal for cooler climates. They are extremely hardy and will stand frosts and cold weather. In fact they improve in taste after a frost. Long after many vegetables have died back, sprouts will still be standing tall waiting for you to gather and eat them. You can pinch out the growing tip before the cold weather to direct the plant's energy into forming sprouts.

Growing

▶ **Sowing:** Sprouts can be sown straight into the ground, although some might need cloches to warm up the soil. You can also sow sprouts in seed trays and transplant them when their roots start to push out of the compost. The time of year depends on when you want to harvest your crop.

▶ **Varieties:** 'Peer Gynt' is one of the most popular varieties.

▶ **Tending:** As long as you keep the newly transplanted crop well watered, sprouts should grow well. Once they are established, they will need watering only during dry spells. Keep them weeded and mulch around them if it is very dry weather.

▶ **Container gardening:** Brussels sprouts are not good for container gardening because they are tall with shallow roots. This means they can topple over in containers.

Protecting

▶ **Pests:** Brussels sprouts may be attacked by birds, so cover plants with netting if necessary. You will need to keep an eye on caterpillars and aphids too.

▶ **Diseases:** Sprouts may be affected by mildew and club root. If they get club root, you will need to dig up the plants and destroy them.

Top Tip

Wait until the first frost to harvest your sprouts as this improves the taste.

Harvesting and Storing

▶ **Harvesting:** Sprouts can be ready from early autumn, depending on the variety, but they are traditionally picked through the winter and, in the UK, are served on Christmas Day. Sprouts tend to improve in flavour after a frost, so leave in the ground as long as you can. Harvest them from the bottom of the stalk upwards.

▶ **Storage:** Brussels sprout stalks will remain in the ground throughout the winter or you can cut the entire stalk and hang it before using. Sprouts freeze well.

Eating

In the UK, most people tolerate Brussels sprouts on Christmas Day as part of a tradition, but many will eat them only once a year. This is a shame because if cooked well, they can be a lovely addition to meals. They are particularly good shredded and stir-fried to retain their crunch and taste. Brussels sprouts are a good match for chestnuts in a traditional side dish and are also a good ingredient for bubble and squeak. Brussels sprouts should never be overcooked; this gives them a dull grey appearance and a bitter taste.

Did You Know?

Cabbage is considered to be one of the greatest healers in the vegetable kingdom.

Cabbages

There are cabbages for every season, varying from loose spring greens to tightly packed red cabbages and the king of cabbages, the Savoy. Cabbages take up a lot of space and can take months to mature, but the rewards are high as they are hardy crops that can be eaten in a variety of ways.

Growing

▶ **Sowing:** Cabbages can be sown outdoors in situ or in seed trays for transplanting later. Sow outdoors in damp drills and thin out when the seedlings appear. When you transplant cabbage plants, water them in well.

▶ **Varieties:** 'Hispi' is a summer favourite, while 'Savoy' has deep green crinkly leaves that are highly nutritious.

198

▶ **Tending:** Provided you water cabbages in well when transplanting, they will need little watering except in very dry spells.

▶ **Container gardening:** Cabbages do better in raised beds than in containers.

Protecting

▶ **Pests:** Protect from the Cabbage White with horticultural fleece and keep an eye open for slugs and snails.

▶ **Diseases:** Watch out for club root and dig up and destroy any affected crops.

Harvesting and Storing

▶ **Harvesting:** Cut the cabbage stem close to the ground with a sharp knife. If you cut a cross into the cabbage stump you'll get a cluster of small heads that you can eat.

▶ **Storage:** Most cabbages can be left in the ground until you need them. Shredded cabbage freezes well. Red cabbage can be pickled and white cabbage can be made into sauerkraut.

Eating

Many people have memories of school cabbage as their least favourite vegetable. However, prepared properly, cabbage can be delicious. Eat cabbage raw with salads or in coleslaw. Finely shred cabbage leaves and steam until tender then serve with butter. Cabbage can be added to potato or vegetable soups and red cabbage takes on a new taste when slow cooked in the oven with butter, sugar, cooking apples and vinegar. The large leaves of Savoy cabbage can be stuffed. And who can resist the ultimate comfort food, bubble and squeak?

Kale

Kale is a great crop for beginners: it is easy to take care of, hardy and, if you harvest it carefully, you can treat it as a cut-and-come-again crop. It can tolerate most soils and conditions, it will grow in some shade and it will provide you with food throughout the winter.

Did You Know?

Kale is the easiest member of the cabbage family for beginners to grow.

Growing

▶ **Sowing:** Seeds germinate quickly; sow them in seedling trays in mid-spring and transplant them a couple of months later. Water the plants thoroughly before moving and water well once you have transplanted them. Firm them into the soil because they can get quite tall and need to be secure.

▶ **Varieties:** 'Frosty', as the name implies, is very hardy, surviving the coldest of winters. 'Dwarf green curled' grows quickly and easily.

▶ **Tending:** Kale is the ideal member of the cabbage family for beginners to grow. It is hardy and will take some neglect. Make sure young plants don't get too dry and keep the weeds away. Remove any yellowing leaves and stake the kale if it is in an exposed place.

▶ **Container gardening:** 'Dwarf green curled' and 'Showbor' are perfect varieties for containers.

Protecting

▶ **Pests:** Kale is rarely bothered by pests, except the Cabbage White butterfly. Use horticultural fleece or netting to prevent eggs being laid.

▶ **Diseases:** Kale will withstand most of the diseases that can attack other members of the cabbage family.

Harvesting and Storing

▶ **Harvesting:** Cut leaves with a sharp knife and leave the plant in the ground to produce new leaves. You should be able to harvest kale throughout the winter.

▶ **Storage:** Kale is better if eaten fresh but does freeze well. You can store it in the refrigerator for a few days.

Eating

Young leaves are tender and can be eaten raw in salads or added to stir-fries. You can steam or boil kale in a little water, then drain and serve with butter or fry it in a little oil with some garlic and spices. You can substitute kale for cabbage in soup recipes, use it in place of cabbage or sprouts in bubble and squeak, or finely shred it and add it to quiches, pies or omelettes.

201

Peas, Beans and Corn

Peas and beans are otherwise known as legumes. They help fix nitrogen in the soil and can help improve it. Peas and beans are suitable for beds and containers. Most beans are easy to grow and produce high yields, although they like warm soil and must not be planted out when there is risk of frost. Sweetcorn is a delightful crop to grow. Although it is not always successful, fresh sweetcorn is sweet and tender; unlike anything you can buy.

Broad Beans

Broad beans will tolerate most soils and conditions, although you might like to enrich the soil during the autumn before planting. Broad beans are the first of the beans to mature and reach your table, giving you a taste of spring.

Top Tip

Make a delicious 'houmous' from broad beans with garlic, seasoning, lemon juice and olive oil.

Growing

▶ **Sowing:** Broad beans can be sown in situ from spring onwards; plant until the end of May for a continual supply. Broad beans are fairly easy going when it comes to soil and conditions and they are a nice crop for beginners because they mature quickly.

▶ **Varieties:** 'Bunyards Exhibition' is an old reliable favourite and 'Red Epicure' gets rave reviews.

▶ **Tending:** Broad beans are great for first-time gardeners. Most varieties don't need staking except in very exposed sites, they help add fertility to the soil and are not too fussy about watering unless it is very dry when the pods are swelling.

▶ **Container gardening:** You can try broad beans in pots but you will probably get a small yield. Try 'The Sutton', which is suited to smaller gardens.

Protecting

▶ **Pests:** Pinching out the tips can help prevent blackfly, which can be a serious pest to broad beans. Mice can be a problem in some areas; the best way to avoid this is to plant beans in seed trays and plant out more mature plants into the soil.

Harvesting and Storing

▶ **Harvesting:** After harvesting the pods, leave the plants in the soil to fix nitrogen before digging into the soil. Pick beans when they are 5–7.5 cm (2–3 in) long as they will be most tender. If you want to pod the beans, wait until you can see the bumps of the beans through the pod.

▶ **Storage:** Broad beans will store for a few days in the fridge and freeze very well. You can dry them in their pods for long-term storage.

203

Eating

Young broad beans can be eaten whole, including the pod. They need minimal cooking time. Older beans can be podded and boiled or steamed for a few minutes. You can leave beans to mature on the plant and then dry them for a winter staple that makes a good addition to hearty soups. Steamed tender broad beans make a great addition to warm salads, especially if served with a creamy cheese. Small beans can be added to risotto. If the tops of the bean plants are in good condition, you can eat these too.

Peas

Peas are worth growing because nothing beats the taste of a freshly podded pea. They are at their best in early summer before temperatures get too hot. In addition to garden peas you will see sugar snap peas, mangetout and petit pois.

Growing

▶ **Sowing:** Peas can provide a long harvesting season if you choose successive crops. Like potatoes, you get earlies, second earlies and main crops. They need rich soil that is kept moist so add compost or manure the autumn before you plan to sow them. Allow the ground to warm up before planting them in situ.

▶ **Varieties:** 'Early Onward' is a good early pea. 'Hurst greenshaft' is a popular disease-resistant maincrop.

Did You Know?

Only about five per cent of the peas sold today are sold fresh; the rest are canned or frozen.

▶ **Tending:** Peas need support. Some varieties grow tall, whereas others are shorter, however all varieties have tendrils that need to wrap around something, so provide netting, sticks or canes. Peas need to be kept moist otherwise they do not form well but it is better to water them well twice a week than a little every day. Keep the soil around plants moist with mulches.

▶ **Container gardening:** 'Kelvedon Wonder' is ideal for containers.

Protecting

▶ **Pests:** Mice and birds can be a problem for peas – they both like the seeds and seedlings – so protect plants with traps and netting. Pea Moth is another pest; reduce the risk by planning planting times to avoid the worst season and by using fleece.

Harvesting and Storing

▶ **Harvesting:** Pick often; you may find yourself with a glut, so eat what you can fresh and store the rest. After you have finished harvesting, leave the plant in the ground and dig in to add nitrogen to the soil.

▶ **Storage:** Try not to store peas in the fridge, pick them as you want to eat them and enjoy them at their peak. Peas freeze exceptionally well.

Eating

Fresh peas are best picked and eaten raw, but if you don't like raw peas then cook them straight away for a few minutes until tender. Serve them with butter and mint. They make excellent soups, either a hearty winter soup or a light summer soup, such as pea, lettuce and mint – a great recipe for making the most of summer gluts. Pea shoots can be eaten too.

Runner Beans

Runner beans (sometimes called string beans) are a great crop for beginners. If you provide rich soil and water them well during dry periods you will be rewarded with a huge crop. They require constant picking through the harvesting season otherwise the plants stop producing beans. Runner beans grow prolifically, so you should grow fewer than you think you will need!

Growing

▶ **Sowing:** Runner beans grow easily. Put two seeds into a seedling cell and when they are bursting out of their pots transplant them into warm, prepared soil.

▶ **Varieties:** 'Scarlet Emperor' is an old favourite with high yields.

▶ **Tending:** Runner beans are easy to maintain, but they require plenty of water when the flowers are forming to produce a good crop. Keep weeds at bay to save them competing for water. Runner beans need something to climb up – rows of wigwams of bamboo canes are a popular choice. Put two beans around one cane and they will wind their way to the top.

▶ **Container gardening:** 'Hestia' is perfect for pots. Plant two rows side by side to support one another.

Protecting

▶ **Pests:** Slugs are fond of runner
bean seedlings; protect against
them with barriers or traps. Mice
can pull up the seeds, but this is
not usually a problem if you start
the beans indoors.

Harvesting and Storing

▶ **Harvesting:** You need to pick
runner beans regularly otherwise
they stop producing new beans.
During the summer you may need
to pick them every day to keep
up with them!

▶ **Storage:** Runner beans store well in the freezer and an old-fashioned method of preservation is
salting. Runner bean chutney is a good recipe to have on hand for dealing with a glut.

Did You Know?

Many varieties of runner
bean can grow to over
1.8 m (6 ft) tall!

Eating

Young runner beans will not have developed tough strings, so you
can chop them up and steam until tender. Older beans might need
stringing before cooking. You can add runner beans to paellas and
risottos or chop finely and put into quiches. Serve them with
a vinaigrette as a salad.

207

Sweetcorn

Sweetcorn is worth growing to get that home-grown experience. Like peas and tomatoes, nothing beats freshly picked sweetcorn for taste and texture – it is quite unlike anything you can buy. Sweetcorn is unfussy about soil conditions, but it needs to drain well and requires a sunny site.

Growing

▶ **Sowing:** Sow seeds indoors in seed trays. Keep potting on until the plant is well established, but don't disturb the roots when transplanting. Once you are sure there will be no more frost, you can plant sweetcorn in its outdoor space. Plant it in blocks, rather than rows, to ensure pollination.

▶ **Varieties:** 'Earlybird' F1 is one of the earliest super-sweet varieties. 'Lark' is extra tender and sweet with golden kernels.

Did You Know?

According to legend, corn is grown with peas and squash as one of the 'three sisters'. Corn provides poles for beans to climb; beans fix nitrogen in the soil and squash suppresses weeds.

▶ **Tending:** Once the weather is warm enough, sweetcorn takes off like Jack's beanstalk and matures surprisingly quickly for such a huge plant. Make sure you water it well after transplanting it and while the kernels are swelling. Keep the area weed free and mulch if necessary.

▶ **Container gardening:** 'Mini Pop', a baby sweetcorn that is good for stir-fries and salad dishes, is suitable for containers.

Harvesting and Storing

▶ **Harvesting:** Sweetcorn is ready for harvesting when the tassels turn brown. You can test for ripeness by sticking your nail in a kernel; it will exude milky liquid when ready. As soon as it is picked, sweetcorn begins to lose its sweetness and tenderness; within seconds the sugars turn to starch. So pick it when you want to eat it, or leave it on the plant for another day. You will get roughly two ears of corn per plant.

▶ **Storage:** It is not a good idea to store sweetcorn as it deteriorates so quickly, but it will keep for a couple of days in the fridge. You can dry sweetcorn and make it into popping corn.

Eating

You will get the best taste from sweetcorn if you bring a pan of water to the boil before you take the sweetcorn from the plant. Snap it off the plant and as you are walking back to your kitchen start to peel back the leaves and silks. By the time you get through the door, you'll be ready to pop the ear of corn into the water and it will be ready in minutes. The best way to eat sweetcorn is slathered with butter and nibbled off the cob!

Salad and Leafy Crops

Gone are the days of limp, tasteless lettuce; there is now a huge number of different salad leaves available. Some are mild, others are peppery, some have a delicate sweet taste while others have bitter qualities. Salad leaves are a great crop for beginners because the rewards are swift. You can be eating your first meal in a few short weeks, and if you sow at intervals you can pick fresh salad every day throughout the year.

Chard and Spinach

Chard is easy to grow and can provide wonderful colour in your garden with its rainbow and ruby-red varieties. It will keep going throughout the winter in all but the harshest climates and is ideal for any sized plot or container. The more you cut it, the more it seems to grow! Spinach is slightly more fussy than chard, but still easy to grow and can be harvested all year round.

Growing

Did You Know?

A bag of supermarket
salad leaves has
used about 50 litres
(13 gallons)
of water to grow.

▶ **Sowing:** You can sow chard seeds in situ in autumn or spring for a cut-and-come-again crop. Thin seedlings when they appear and put the thinnings in your salad. Chard likes fertile soil. If you want to grow large leaves you can sow seeds in seed trays and transplant them into your prepared soil later. Sow spinach leaf seeds in situ in cooler weather during spring and winter as they won't germinate in hot weather.

▶ **Chard Varieties:** 'Bright Lights' provides a wonderful array of colour and is suitable for beds or containers.

▶ **Spinach Varieties:** 'Toscane' is slow to bolt and produces high yields. 'Medania' can be sown for both summer and winter harvesting.

▶ **Tending:** Make sure chard doesn't get too dry otherwise it can bolt, but it can withstand some neglect and still look and taste great. Spinach will sulk if conditions are not right: it needs nutritionally rich soil with plenty of water. Don't allow the soil around spinach to dry out; use mulches if necessary. Spinach can bolt in hot weather; if it does so you'll have to remove the plants.

▶ **Container gardening:** Both chard and spinach are ideal for containers. Spinach 'Tirza' is good for baby spinach leaves.

Protecting

▶ **Pests:** Slugs love the soft leaves of most types and will munch through your chard seedlings. Protect them with traps or barriers. Birds can be a pest too; cover the plants with netting to prevent damage.

Harvesting and Storing

▶ **Harvesting:** Chard and spinach will be ready to eat within two to three months of sowing. Cut off the leaves you want to eat with a sharp knife and more will grow in its place. Smaller leaves can be eaten raw, while larger leaves can be lightly cooked.

▶ **Storage:** Chard and spinach will store for a few days in the fridge, especially if you store like cut flowers – with the stems in a glass of water. Both can also be frozen.

Eating

Small leaves can be added raw to a salad to provide interest and colour. Slightly larger leaves can be 'just cooked' in stir-fries, while larger leaves lend themselves to gentle cooking – wash the leaves, shake off excess water and simmer for a few minutes until wilted. Add finely chopped chard or spinach to quiches or add to soups, stews or curries at the last minute.

Lamb's Lettuce and Rocket

Did You Know?
Romans ate rocket for good luck.

Lamb's lettuce (or 'corn salad') deserves a special mention because it provides succulent leaves from November to January when most other salad leaves have finished. Rocket is another easy-to-grow leaf suitable for beginners. It, too, will last through the autumn months and into a mild winter. Lamb's lettuce is mild whereas rocket is more peppery.

Growing

▶ **Sowing:** Lamb's lettuce is tolerant of most soil types. Sow in situ during August and September in drills. Thin out the seedlings and use them in your salad. You can also try growing it indoors in an unheated greenhouse throughout the winter. Sow rocket in situ during spring for a summer crop and autumn for a winter crop. Rocket needs moisture-retentive soil. Lamb's lettuce can be quite slow to grow, whereas you can be eating rocket six weeks after sowing.

▶ **Tending:** Lamb's lettuce needs little attention; keep weeds away when you first plant it and it will keep growing throughout the winter, surviving all but the harshest conditions. Keep the seedlings moist, but don't over water. Rocket can bolt in hot weather, so try sowing it during the autumn and harvest throughout the winter, or choose a shadier site to grow it. Keep it well watered during hot weather to prevent it bolting or becoming too peppery.

▶ **Container gardening:** Lamb's lettuce and rocket are both suitable for growing in containers.

Protecting

▶ **Pests:** Birds and slugs are the main problems for lamb's lettuce, but it is generally easy to grow. Slugs will eat rocket; protect it with barriers or traps.

Harvesting and Storing

▶ **Harvesting:** Harvest lamb's lettuce during the winter. Cut the leaves you want with a pair of scissors and leave the rest of the plant in the ground to produce more leaves. Rocket will provide leaves during summer and winter, depending on when you sow it. Harvest it in the same way as lamb's lettuce.

Did You Know?

Lamb's lettuce gets its name because it resembles the size and shape of a lamb's tongue!

213

▶ **Storage:** Lamb's lettuce and rocket will store for a few days in the fridge in an airtight container, but both are best eaten fresh.

Eating

Both leaves are mainly eaten raw in salads. They can be used in place of lettuce to add more interest to side salads or as the base for a main-meal salad. The leaves work well in sandwiches. Rocket can be added to soups, chopped into omelettes and couscous or used in place of basil for pesto. Lamb's lettuce can be cooked like spinach and served as a side vegetable.

Lettuce

There are many types of lettuce, ranging from red-tipped, curly-leaved lollo rossa to dense green heads. You will also come across cos, loose-leaf, butterhead and crisphead varieties. Crisphead, butterhead and cos lettuces produce a heart, a bit like a cabbage, whereas loose-leaf ones are a mass of frilly leaves. You can take just the leaves you need from loose-leaf varieties, so they are perfect if you don't eat much salad or there is only one lettuce-lover in your home.

Growing

▶ **Sowing:** Sow lettuce seeds in situ on a sunny site and in fertile soil or plant in the plants are big enough. You can thin seedlings to get larger lettuces or leave looser-leaved lettuces packed more densely for cut-and-come-again leaves. It is important to stagger your sowing, otherwise you'll end up with a glut of lettuces, which will be wasted. Try to sow seeds at weekly intervals for a continual crop.

Did You Know?

Lettuce leaves can be used as an external poultice for inflamed swellings and bruises.

▶ **Varieties:** 'Webs Wonder' is popular and less likely than some other varieties to bolt in hot weather. 'Lollo Rossa' is a loose-leaf lettuce with a striking red colour.

▶ **Tending:** Lettuces can bolt quickly in hot weather. You can help prevent this by mulching around your crop and ensuring the plants get enough water. Keep the soil moist and weed regularly. Lettuces have shallow roots, so make sure your soil is nutrient rich.

▶ **Container gardening:** 'Tom Thumb' and 'Little Gem' are ideal for containers.

Protecting

▶ **Pests:** Aphids can be a problem; keep an eye on your plants and rub off aphids with your finger. Attracting ladybirds to your garden helps because they eat aphids. Slugs enjoy tender lettuce seedlings; you will need to deter them with barriers or set up traps.

Harvesting and Storing

▶ **Harvesting:** When the lettuce is ready, cut it from the stem and leave the stem in the ground where you will get fresh leaves. It is important to use the lettuce once it has reached maturity because it can bolt within a week.

▶ **Storage:** Lettuces will store in the refrigerator for a few days, but it's best if you harvest what you need at the time. You can prolong the life of lettuce by storing leaves in a box of cold water in the fridge – they can last for up to a week like this.

Eating

Although mainly eaten in salads, lettuce can be cooked. It's an idea to grow a variety of lettuces and take a few leaves of each for a mixed salad base. Lettuce leaves can be used to fill sandwiches and pitta breads. Large lettuce leaves can be used like taco shells or 'spring rolls' – stuff with bean sprouts and thinly sliced carrots. Little Gem lettuces can be barbecued; cut them in half lengthways, brush with oil and grill then serve with vinaigrette. For people who hate lettuce, you can disguise them in purées and soups. You can also braise lettuce for a couple of minutes with onions and garlic.

Mizuna and Mustard

Mizuna is an Oriental vegetable with serrated leaves that has a mild mustard flavour and can be eaten raw or cooked. It is easy to grow and some people grow it as a pretty 'wild flower' in their borders. Mustard, which develops yellow flowers quickly in hot weather, has a more pungent taste. Salad-leaf mixes, particularly ones labelled 'spicy', often contain mizuna and mustard leaves.

Growing

▶ **Sowing:** Sow mizuna and mustard *in situ* from late spring to late summer for a continual crop. You can also sow it indoors for a winter cut-and-come-again crop. Mizuna and mustard will tolerate both full sun and light shade.

▶ **Tending:** Mizuna and mustard are adaptable plants that grow
well in most soils, but keep plants moist to prevent them
bolting. Weed well and use mulches if necessary.

▶ **Container gardening:** Both mizuna and mustard are ideal for
growing in containers.

Harvesting and Storing

▶ **Harvesting:** Mizuna is quick growing: you can be eating it as little as three weeks after sowing.
Cut the leaves you want to eat with scissors. Harvest mustard leaves before the flowers grow and
pull up the plants before the flowers drop their seeds otherwise it will grow like a weed all over
your garden!

▶ **Storage:** Mizuna and mustard leaves will store in the fridge in an airtight container for a few days,
but are best eaten fresh.

Protecting

▶ **Pests:** Slugs will eat young seedlings; prevent
them with barriers and traps.

Eating

Mizuna and mustard leaves are usually eaten raw
in salads and mizuna is often cooked in stir-fries.
Mizuna lends itself to Oriental dishes and is good
when dressed with sesame oil.

Gourd Family

The gourd family includes cucumbers, courgettes, pumpkins and squashes. They are relatively trouble free to grow but need a lot of space, so are not ideal for very small gardens, though you might manage one courgette or cucumber plant. Some people grow the plants vertically if ground space is in short supply. All members of the gourd family grow rapidly and they can be prolific croppers in fertile soil.

Cucumber

There are both indoor and outdoor cucumbers. Outdoor cucumbers are easier to grow and require less attention. The harvesting season is short so some gardeners feel it is not worth the effort to grow their own cucumbers.

Growing

▶ **Sowing:** Outdoor cucumbers can be sown in situ when the weather is warm – mid to late spring is ideal. They like rich soil, so dig a hole and fill it with compost before popping in a couple of seeds. Cucumbers like warmth to germinate; put a cloche over the seed to keep the soil warm if necessary. Select the strongest seedling and thin out the weaker one. Indoor cucumbers usually germinate well. Start them off in small pots and move to larger pots when the plants are established.

▶ **Varieties:** 'Burpless Tasty Green' is suitable for outdoor growing; 'Femspot', which is highly resistant to disease, is good for greenhouses.

▶ **Tending:** Keep the soil warm and moist, especially while the fruit is forming. You can allow outdoor cucumbers to snake along the ground or support them with sticks. They are quite hungry plants and you may need to feed them with an all-purpose fertilizer while the fruits are growing. Indoor cucumbers can get too dry: make sure they have plenty of water and humidity and give them some form of support to climb up.

▶ **Container gardening:** 'Green Finger' is a baby cucumber – wonderful for children to grow. 'Mini Munch' can be harvested when small or left to grow large.

Protecting

▶ **Pests:** Slugs are fond of young cucumber plants; repel them with barriers or traps.

▶ **Diseases:** If conditions are too damp, cucumber plants can suffer from powdery mildew.

Harvesting and Storing

Did You Know?

Cucumber slices really are good for the eyes: cucumbers have cooling and anti-inflammatory properties.

▶ **Harvesting:** When the cucumbers are large enough, cut them off with a sharp knife. Harvest them regularly to encourage new growth on the plant. If you let them mature, the plant will stop growing new cucumbers.

▶ **Storage:** Although best eaten fresh, cucumbers store well in the refrigerator for a week or two. Gherkins can be pickled.

Eating

Cucumbers are eaten raw, usually sliced and served with salad. You can chop them finely and add to yogurt as a dip or curry accompaniment and they are one of the main ingredients of tabbouleh. Cucumbers can be diced and made into salsa or shredded with a vegetable peeler for a raw version of spaghetti. Cucumber sandwiches are the perfect summer afternoon tea and you can serve long sticks of cucumber with dips for crudités. Cucumbers are one of the ingredients in the Spanish chilled soup gazpacho. Some people cook them, but they go soft very quickly.

Courgettes and Marrows

If you want a crop that is prolific and easy to grow, then courgettes are the answer. Although the harvesting season is relatively short, most families need only one or two plants to benefit from a glut of food! Courgettes like a sunny site and fertile soil.

Growing

▶ **Sowing:** Courgettes can be planted in situ in large pots, grow bags or directly into the soil. Fill a hole with compost and put in the seeds. Leave plenty of room for the plants to grow if you are sowing into the ground. You can also sow indoors and transplant later in the year.

Top Tip

Keep the stems on pumpkins if you want to store them as they deteriorate faster once the stem is removed.

▶ **Varieties:** 'Zucchini' are best picked when small and tender. 'Jaguar' have dark green skins and an excellent flavour.

▶ **Tending:** As long as courgettes are kept moist they are fairly unfussy. Mulching can help keep the soil moist. Inconsistent watering may lead to odd-shaped fruits. Courgettes are hungry crops; you can feed them with fertilizer when the fruits are swelling.

▶ **Container gardening:** Even though the plants can grow very large, courgettes do well in large pots filled with compost.

Protecting

▶ **Pests:** Slugs enjoy young courgette plants; either deter these pests with barriers or traps or raise the plants indoors and plant them out when they are larger.

▶ **Diseases:** Keep the fruits off the ground when they are forming to prevent them rotting. Courgettes can get powdery mildew; if they do, make sure you keep the soil moist and use a fungicide.

Harvesting and Storing

▶ **Harvesting:** Harvest courgettes when they are small for best results. Cut them with a sharp knife from the stem; if you try to pull or twist them off you can damage both the fruit and the plant. You will need to check plants daily as courgettes can turn to marrows overnight! If you want marrows, leave them until they are the right size, but bear in mind that if they get too big, the plant will stop producing new fruit.

221

▶ **Storage:** Once picked, courgettes will store in the refrigerator for up to a week. Marrows will store for longer in a cool place. Both can be made into chutney.

Eating

Young courgettes are delicious when steamed for a few minutes before serving. They are creamy without any of the bitterness associated with older crops. Courgettes can be sliced finely and stir-fried, made into creamy soups or used as an ingredient for ratatouille or summer casseroles. Dice them and add to risottos or slice thinly with a vegetable peeler and use in place of spaghetti. The flowers can be stuffed and deep-fried. Marrows are traditionally scooped out and stuffed or turned into chutneys and pickles.

Squash and Pumpkins

There are many types of winter squash, the most common being acorn, butternut and spaghetti squash. They are lovely to see in the garden with their various shapes, sizes and colours. You will need to choose an appropriate variety for the size of your garden: one pumpkin plant can take over an entire raised bed! Give each plant plenty of room to sprawl.

Growing

▶ **Sowing:** Squashes and pumpkins are usually planted *in situ* on mounds of compost. In fact, you can grow squashes successfully in your compost heap, where they will soak up the warmth and nutrients. You may need to warm up the soil before sowing. If you want to get a head start, then sow the seeds indoors and transplant when the ground is warm and all risks of frost have passed. Use cloches if the weather turns cold.

222

▶ **Varieties:** 'Sweet Dumpling' and 'Hunter' are two good varieties to try.

▶ **Tending:** Squashes and pumpkins need warm soil and sunlight to thrive; they will not germinate in cold conditions. Pumpkins are very thirsty plants. When the fruits are growing you can feed them with an all-purpose fertilizer or continue to mulch them with compost. Once the leaves are growing, they provide their own ground cover to prevent water evaporation from the soil. You might need to take some fruits off each vine otherwise they will be competing for food. For best results, leave just one or two pumpkins or three or four squashes on a vine.

▶ **Container gardening:** Squashes and pumpkins are not really suitable for containers, although you might manage an acorn squash in a large pot.

Protecting

▶ **Pests:** Slugs will eat young plants and the fruits themselves; set up barriers or traps to prevent this.

▶ **Diseases:** Squashes and pumpkins can get powdery mildew, which is a fungal infection. Use a fungicide and ensure moist soil at all times to prevent a reoccurrence. The fruits can rot too. Prevent this by keeping them up off the soil; mounds of hay or an old brick are ideal.

Did You Know?

Pumpkin seeds are full of zinc, which is important for prostate health. Men can eat 10 pumpkin seeds a day to help prevent prostate problems.

Harvesting and Storing

▶ **Harvesting:** You can cut pumpkins and squashes for immediate use off the vine with a sharp knife. If you want to store them for winter food you will need to 'cure' them. This means leaving them on the plant to develop a tough protective skin. Cut from the vine when ready, leaving as long a stalk as possible, and put in a warm place for a week or two before storing in a cool place.

▶ **Storage:** Pumpkins and squashes store well. You can hang them in nets to allow air to circulate between them. Alternatively, cut the flesh into cubes and freeze for later use.

Eating

Small squash can be baked whole and the flesh scooped out. Spaghetti squash can indeed be used as a spaghetti substitute: bake it then shred the flesh with a fork. Squash are lovely when cut into cubes, tossed in oil and roasted in the oven. Pumpkins lend themselves to both sweet and savoury dishes and are traditionally made into soups or sweet pies. And don't forget the seeds! Scoop out the pumpkin seeds, spread thinly on a tray and leave to dry for a few days before storing in an airtight container.

Onion Family

Members of the onion family are popular garden crops. The family includes chives, garlic, leeks, shallots, spring (or salad) onions and a wide variety of onions from red to white.

Garlic

Garlic is easy to grow and very rewarding; each clove planted into the soil will produce a new bulb within a few months.

Growing

▶ **Sowing:** Garlic likes sun to develop large bulbs. Plant cloves in early autumn for an early summer harvest. Choose well-drained but moisture-retentive soil, separate a garlic bulb into individual cloves and pop each clove, sharp end up, into a hole. Push the cloves down until the tip is an inch or two below the soil. Water in, mulch and leave.

▶ **Tending:** Garlic is easy to grow, just keep the area free of weeds and don't let the ground get too wet otherwise the bulbs may rot. There is no need to water garlic throughout the winter, but once spring arrives you can water the bulbs to help them develop. Ease off watering while the bulbs are maturing otherwise they may rot. If your soil is too wet, plant garlic in spring for a late summer to autumn harvest.

▶ **Container gardening:** Garlic grows well in containers with free-draining soil.

Did You Know?

Garlic and leeks are powerful immune-boosting foods. According to an old saying, 'Eat leeks in March and garlic in May, and all the year after physicians may play'.

Protecting

▶ **Pests:** Cloves can be uprooted by pests.

▶ **Diseases:** Garlic bulbs can become mouldy if the weather is damp or the soil does not drain well.

Harvesting and Storing

▶ **Harvesting:** Garlic is ready when the leaves begin to shrivel. Pull up the bulbs and leave them somewhere warm to dry, preferably hung in the full sun. The bulbs are ready when the skin is papery.

▶ **Storage:** Garlic can be plaited and hung somewhere cool and dry.

Eating

Garlic is used as a flavouring in both raw and cooked dishes. Garlic bulbs can be roasted whole and the cloves popped out of their skins and mashed. This results in much creamier and milder tasting garlic, which can be added to soups. Put a couple of cloves of garlic in with roast vegetables, or smash two cloves, mix with butter and spread on French stick for garlic bread.

Leeks

Leeks are worth growing if you have the space, but they take up a lot of room in small gardens. They are a lovely crop to grow because they provide winter food when other food is scarce. Once established, they are easy to take care of, but they can be more difficult to plant properly. Leeks are sown in pots and transplanted.

Growing

▶ **Sowing:** Choose a site that does not become waterlogged, as leeks stand in the soil throughout the winter. Sow seeds indoors in midwinter and get ready to transplant them mid spring when the ground has warmed up. If you're not that organized, sow seeds in spring ready for transplanting in the summer and harvesting in the autumn. When the plants are about as thick as a pencil, they are ready to transplant. Make a hole in your prepared soil, drop a seedling in and fill the hole with water rather than soil.

▶ **Varieties:** 'Edison' can be picked as a baby vegetable or left to mature; 'Musselburgh' is an old favourite.

▶ **Tending:** Once growing, leeks are relatively maintenance free. Keep weeds at bay and you will need to water only during very dry weather. You can earth up leeks as they develop to encourage long white shafts.

▶ **Container gardening:** Try baby varieties such as 'Volta' F1 and 'King Richard'.

227

Protecting

▶ **Pests:** Leeks repel carrot fly.

Harvesting and Storing

▶ **Harvesting:** Pull leeks up as you need them.

▶ **Storage:** Leeks will store well in the refrigerator for a few weeks. Otherwise pull them up, prepare and freeze them.

Eating

Leeks are creamy and mild – a comforting winter vegetable. If you don't like the taste of onions, you may prefer leeks. Leek and potato soup is a satisfying and frugal winter meal. Leeks can be sliced and added to stir-fries and are lovely in macaroni or cauliflower cheese. You can roast them too.

Onions and Shallots

Onions and shallots are easy to grow from onion sets (small onion bulbs that have been pre-started into growth before sale). You can grow them from seeds, but sets are ideal for beginners. Onions form the base of many meals, so it is worth growing some of your own if you have the space. Shallots have a more refined taste, sweeter and milder with a hint of garlic and without any acidity. Both need well-draining soil that does not become waterlogged.

228

Growing

▶ **Sowing:** Sow shallot sets at the beginning of spring in prepared soil. Simply push a set down into the ground until the tip is just showing above the ground. Onion sets can be planted a little later, from mid spring.

▶ **Varieties:** 'Picasso' is a perfect shallot for pickling, while 'Jermor' is good for cooking. 'Red Baron' is a lovely red onion and 'Sturon' is good for storing.

▶ **Tending:** Weed regularly around plants to prevent weeds competing for water and nutrients. Onions need moisture-retentive soil but must never get too wet. Mulching around crops will cut down on the watering you need to do.

▶ **Container gardening:** Spring onions and shallots are suitable for containers.

Did You Know?

Research has shown that onions have anti-bacterial properties and can help with respiratory, digestive and urinary infections.

Protecting

▶ **Pests:** Birds can pull onion sets out of the ground; deter them from the area with netting. Onions can also suffer from onion fly. Use horticultural fleece to prevent tunnelling maggots from rotting the crop.

▶ **Diseases:** Onions and shallots are pretty much disease free but they can get mildew or mould.

229

Harvesting and Storing

▶ **Harvesting:** Onions and shallots are ready to harvest when their foliage begins to turn yellow. Loosen soil around the bulbs with a fork, then pull them up and leave them in the sun to dry for a few days. You will need to separate the shallots into individual bulbs before drying them to allow air to circulate.

▶ **Storage:** Look for onions with longer storage times if you want to keep them. Once dried, hang them up – in nets or old tights or tied in strings – in a cool, dry place. Onions and shallots freeze well and can be pickled.

Eating

Spring onions are eaten raw in salads or chopped and added to stir-fries. Shallots have a milder and creamier taste than onions and are delicious in winter stews and casseroles. Onions have many culinary uses: you can eat them raw in salads and they are a basic ingredient in most meals, including pies, soups and stews. Onion soup is a warming winter dish.

Soft Vegetables

This section includes aubergines, peppers and tomatoes – softer vegetables that need warmer conditions to grow. All will grow outdoors in a sheltered, sunny spot, but are better grown in a greenhouse in the UK. They are useful to grow if you want to save money on your food bill as they are some of the more expensive foods to buy. They will provide a good harvest throughout the summer months – in time for some Mediterranean-style feasting!

Top Tip

Some aubergines can be bitter. To prevent this, cut the aubergine into slices, sprinkle with salt and leave for 30 minutes to draw out the bitter juices before rinsing off salt and cooking.

Aubergines

Aubergines are gaining in popularity. They produce a beautiful sight of different size, colour and shaped fruits. The most popular are the deep purple glossy ones. They need to be grown in a sunny, sheltered spot and ideally indoors unless your climate is very warm and steady.

Growing

▶ **Sowing:** Aubergines need fertile, well-drained soil. Sow them indoors, in seedling trays of seed compost, and transplant when the second leaves appear. If you want to grow them outside, make sure the soil is really warm before sowing; you can use cloches to warm up the soil. Planting in containers will ensure the soil heats up well. Once the plants are established, give them something to grow against, such as a stake.

► **Varieties:** 'Black Beauty' gives a bumper crop.

► **Tending:** Aubergines like humidity; keep the compost moist and use an all-purpose fertilizer every 10 days or so as the fruits set. Depending on the size fruits you want, you will need to take some off the plants: leave around five for large fruits and more for mini aubergines.

► **Container gardening:** Aubergines grow well in containers on a sunny windowsill or in a conservatory. Bushy dwarf varieties, such as 'Baby Bell', are suitable for a sunny, sheltered outdoor spot.

Protecting

► **Pests:** The red spider mite can be a problem for aubergines. Keep these pests at bay by ensuring that plants remain humid. Aphids, too, can attack aubergine plants. Remove individual aphids from the plants with your fingers or, in the case of an infestation, blast them off with jets of water.

► **Diseases:** Botrytis can occur if humidity is too high; prevent it by maintaining good air circulation around the plants.

Harvesting and Storing

► **Harvesting:** When they are ready to be picked, cut the stem with a sharp knife, leaving an inch or so of the stem intact.

Top Tip
Bake aubergines whole then mash or purée the flesh with olive oil, lemon juice and herbs to make a dip.

▶ **Storage:** Aubergines last only a few days once picked, so it is better to pick them as you need them. They can be preserved in chutneys.

Eating

Ratatouille is a popular dish made with aubergines; batch cook and freeze it for later use. To make delicious pâtés from aubergines, coat them in oil and roast them, then blend the flesh together with fried shallots and garlic. You can roast cubed aubergines in oil and they are delicious in vegetable curries. Another popular aubergine dish is moussaka. Aubergines can also be cut in half lengthways and stuffed, in the same way as marrows.

Peppers

Peppers (capsicum) are best grown indoors; a deep windowsill is ideal if you don't have a greenhouse. Peppers include the sweet bell peppers as well as hot, fiery chillies.

Growing

▶ **Sowing:** Unless your plot is very warm and sheltered, you will probably have more success growing peppers and chillies indoors. Peppers need moisture-retentive but freely draining soil. Sow seeds in seed compost in early spring and transplant when big enough into larger pots or grow bags.

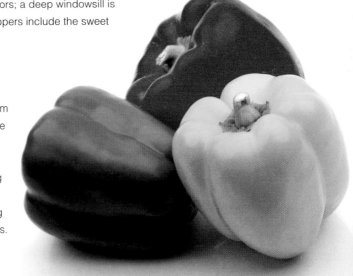

▶ **Varieties:** 'Sweet Chocolate' makes an interesting crop with its chocolate-colour skin. Otherwise look for a mixed seed pack of different varieties and colours.

▶ **Tending:** Peppers need regular and frequent watering, especially when the fruits are setting. Stake the plants to prevent the stems from breaking. Ensure a good balance of humidity and ventilation.

Did You Know?
Green peppers contain twice the amount of vitamin C as citrus fruits.

▶ **Container gardening:** Peppers are suitable for growing in large containers or grow bags and you may manage to grow them outdoors in a very sheltered, sunny site.

Protecting

▶ **Pests:** Prevent red spider mite with good ventilation. Peppers require humidity, so you'll need to keep an eye on things to make sure you have the balance right. Aphids can be a problem too; watch your plants for any sign of infestation.

Harvesting and Storing

▶ **Harvesting:** Leaving your first peppers to mature on the stems will prevent the production of further fruit. Pick the first ones when they are green and allow some of the later crop to fully ripen if you want red peppers, which are sweeter than the green ones. Cut the peppers from the plant, leaving a small stem; don't try to pull them off or you may damage the plant.

▶ **Storage:** Peppers are delicious when eaten fresh as they are crisp and juicy. They will last for a week or more in the refrigerator, but wrinkle quickly once cut. If you have a glut, you can freeze them for adding to cooked dishes later on. Chillies can be eaten fresh or dried. Dry them by hanging the entire plant upside down in an airy, warm place.

Eating

Peppers can be eaten raw or cooked. They can be cut up in salads or stuffed and baked in the oven. Long strips or rings of pepper can be added to stir-fries, and diced peppers in a variety of colours are lovely in vegetarian chillies and curries. Sweet peppers are delicious when skewered and barbecued or cut into long strips and served as crudités. Chillies are used in any dish that needs a fiery kick.

Tomatoes

Tomatoes are one of the most popular home-grown crops. Once you get the hang of it, tomatoes are relatively easy to grow, especially if you have a greenhouse. They will grow outdoors, but need heat and dry weather to produce a good yield. There is a wide variety from which to choose, ranging from plum tomatoes, which lend themselves to cooking, and beefsteak, which are ideal for stuffing, to the popular cherry tomatoes, which are perfect in salads.

Growing

▶ **Sowing:** Tomatoes need fertile soil and growing them in containers of compost or grow bags is ideal for beginners. Sow in seed trays of seed compost indoors during early spring. Prick out and put in larger pots until they are about 20 cm (8 in) tall, when they will be ready to be planted in their final place. If you want to transplant them outdoors, wait until all chance of frost has passed and the soil is warm.

> **Did You Know?**
> As a member of the nightshade family, tomatoes were once thought to be poisonous, so were grown only for decoration.

▶ **Varieties:** 'Gardener's Delight' lives up to its name with its lovely texture and taste. 'Big Boy' produces huge tasty beefsteak tomatoes.

▶ **Tending:** Tomatoes, especially those grown indoors, need plenty of water; mulching can help prevent too much moisture loss. Tomatoes will need something to climb against, such as a stick or cane. Once the plants reach about 1.5 m (5 ft), pinch out the tips to divert their energy into developing fruit rather than more leaves. When the fruits are setting, feed with a liquid tomato feed.

▶ **Container gardening:** Tomatoes are ideal container plants. You can grow them in pots, grow bags and even hanging baskets. 'Sweet Million' is ideal for containers and 'Tumbler' is perfect for hanging baskets.

Protecting

▶ **Pests:** Aphids and whitefly can be a problem; ensure a good balance of humidity and ventilation to help keep pests at bay.

▶ **Diseases:** A black circle on the base of the fruit is a sign of blossom end rot. This is a calcium deficiency and is usually caused by insufficient watering. Blight can affect crops; the leaves develop brown or black spots that move to the stems and destroy the fruit. Outdoor tomatoes are more prone to this problem than those grown indoors; a fungicide may help.

Did You Know?

Tomatoes are actually
a fruit and not a vegetable.

Harvesting and Storing

▶ **Harvesting:** Tomatoes are ready for harvesting when they turn red (although some varieties are yellow, orange, purple, white or striped). Gently pull from the plant, taking the calyx as well; if both come away easily in your hand, the fruit is ripe.

▶ **Storage:** Tomatoes are best eaten fresh, but will store for a few days at room temperature. It is best not to store them in the refrigerator as this alters their taste. Gluts can be preserved in the freezer or made into chutneys. If you still have unripe fruits on the vines when frost threatens, dig up the whole plant and hang it somewhere warm where the crop will gradually ripen. Alternatively, pick the green fruits for green tomato chutney.

Eating

Tomatoes are such a versatile ingredient that it's worth growing at least one variety. Cherry tomatoes are best eaten fresh from the vine with salads. Plum tomatoes can be cooked down into pasta sauces and are usually low in acid, which makes them sweeter. Beefsteak tomatoes hold their shape well and can be scooped out, stuffed and baked in the oven. You can make both red and green tomato chutneys, soups or pasta sauces.

237

Root Crops

There are many root crops. This section deals with beetroot, carrot, potatoes and radishes – some of the more common root crops, and some of the easiest for beginners to grow.

Beetroot

Beetroot is a delicious root vegetable producing deep purple globes (although golden, white, oval and long beetroot are also available) that you can harvest at any size you wish. Many people have experienced only pickled beetroot and don't realize that fresh beetroot has a mild, sweet taste. Beetroot can be eaten raw or cooked.

Growing

▶ **Sowing:** You can sow beetroot *in situ* into warm soil. It likes a sunny site with well-drained, fertile soil. If your soil is cold, protect the soil with cloches to warm it up. Sow the seeds in early spring. If your soil needs it, dig compost into it the autumn before you plant.

▶ **Varieties:** 'Boltardy' is a popular variety that is slow to run to seed. 'Burpees Golden' is tender and sweet tasting.

▶ **Tending:** Beetroot requires little attention once the seedlings appear. Keep the soil moist to encourage germination but, once the plants are established, you will need to water only every 10 days or so unless the weather is particularly dry.

▶ **Container gardening:** Small globe varieties are suitable for pots: 'Pablo' F1 and 'Detroit 2' are ideal.

Harvesting and Storing

▶ **Harvesting:** Beetroot can be harvested in as little as 10 weeks; the bulbs will start to push out of the ground when ready.

▶ **Storage:** You can store beetroot in the refrigerator for a couple of weeks. Twist off the leaves and leave a about an inch attached to the root. Beetroot stores well in boxes of sand. It can also be pickled or stored in a clamp.

Protecting

Beetroot seedlings are very attractive to birds, so protect them with nylon netting. Other than that, they are relatively pest- and disease-free.

Eating

Young beetroot can be grated raw into salads. Small beetroot are best boiled with their skins on; once they are tender, remove the skins. Beetroot soup is a popular dish and there are many recipe variations. One of the best ways to serve beetroot is baked. Put it into a foil parcel with a clove of garlic and some butter, wrap it up and place in a hot oven until tender. Alternatively, cut it into large chunks, toss in oil and roast with other vegetables. You can treat the leaves like spinach.

239

Carrots

Home-grown carrots are totally different to those offered for sale in supermarkets. If you have the right soil, carrots are easy to grow but, even if your soil is less than perfect, it is worth persevering, just to be able to savour that freshly picked taste.

Growing

▶ **Sowing:** Carrots love sandy soil and will struggle to grow in damp clay. It is often easier to plant carrots in containers of soil prepared to specification. Sow as thinly as possible during early spring into damp soil, but ensure the soil is warm first. You can harvest carrots nearly all year round if you choose different varieties and sow successionally. To sow seeds thinly, mix them with a little sand before sprinkling with your fingers.

▶ **Varieties:** Choose stump-rooted or round varieties, such as 'Scarlet Horn', for heavier soils. 'Flyaway' is particularly resistant to carrot fly.

▶ **Tending:** Carrots need to be thinned out if you are unable to sow thinly enough and it is at this time that carrot fly can strike. Be very gentle so as not to bruise the leaves and choose a cool, damp day. Carrots need minimal water and sudden watering can cause the roots to split. Keep weeds at bay, by mulching for instance.

▶ **Container gardening:** Short-rooted carrots are ideal for large containers; you can get the soil just right so that they can push down and grow easily. 'Patio Parmex' can be grown in window boxes and even grow bags.

Did You Know?

Perhaps carrots really can help you see in the dark! They are rich in beta-carotene, which is converted into vitamin A. A deficiency of vitamin A can cause night blindness.

Protecting

▶ **Pests:** Carrot flies can damage your crop. They lay eggs and the maggots burrow down into the roots and damage them. You can prevent carrot fly by using horticultural fleece or by planting onions or garlic close by to throw carrot fly off the scent.

Harvesting and Storing

▶ **Harvesting:** Carrots take around three months to reach maturity. Pull them up gently by hand; they should slip out of the soil.

▶ **Storage:** The best place for storing carrots is in the soil. If this is not possible they can be stored in clamps or boxes of sand. Carrots freeze well.

Eating

Carrots lend themselves to both sweet and savoury dishes. Who can resist a slice of carrot cake with rich icing on top? Carrot and coriander soup is a favourite of many. Carrots can be eaten raw in salad, grated into coleslaw or stir-fried. If you want to cook them, using a steamer is ideal as they retain their bite and nutrients. Carrots can also be cut into large chunks and roasted with other root vegetables.

Potatoes

Potatoes are easy enough for children to grow, especially if you stick to earlies (new potatoes), which are less at risk from blight and pests. Potatoes require minimal attention and have the added bonus of conditioning the soil for you. They are an ideal first crop for a newly prepared plot of land as they break up the soil.

Growing

▶ **Sowing:** It is simple to grow potatoes from potato sets in virtually any soil. It is traditional to 'chit' potatoes, which means putting them in shallow trays with the largest number of eyes upwards in a cool, frost-free, light place. Put potatoes into trenches or holes during mid spring for earlies, and late spring for maincrop and cover them with soil so that they are 2.5 cm (1 in) below the surface.

▶ **Varieties:** 'Charlotte' is a creamy, waxy new potato, ideal in salads. 'Rocket' is a white early with big yields. Red 'Desirée' is a good all-rounder maincrop. 'Maris Piper' is a white maincrop, a great roaster.

▶ **Tending:** Potatoes require little attention apart from earthing up, which is necessary to prevent them turning green. To earth up, draw soil from around the plants and cover as much of them as possible. Do this two or three times as the potatoes grow. If your soil is very free draining, then water when the flowers appear to swell the tubers. If you have clay soil, you may not need to water at all.

▶ **Container gardening:** Even though they take up a lot of space in the ground, potatoes can be grown in large pots and stacking tubs – old car tyres are ideal. Try 'Pink Fir' or 'Charlotte'.

Protecting

▶ **Pests:** Slugs and wireworms are more likely to cause problems on maincrop potatoes.

▶ **Diseases:** Blight can affect potatoes if the weather is warm and humid, although you are less likely to encounter it with earlies. If you notice in time, you can use a fungicide, but you need to act quickly and remove affected leaves and stems.

Did You Know?

In October 1995 the potato became the first vegetable to be grown in space.

Harvesting and Storing

▶ **Harvesting:** Early potatoes are ready as soon as the flowers appear. Maincrops are ready when the flowers die and the stems wilt. Fork around the plants and dig up the treasures with your hands to prevent damaging the potatoes. Early potatoes can be eaten straight away. With maincrop potatoes, remove the plants and leave the potatoes in the soil for a couple of weeks before lifting and leaving to dry.

▶ **Storage:** Early potatoes can be stored indoors for a couple of days but need to be eaten before they go green. Dry maincrop potatoes can be stored in hessian sacks in a frost-free place, but they must be completely dry before you store them.

Eating

Potatoes are one of the most versatile vegetables: they can be boiled, steamed, baked, fried, mashed, chipped or roasted. New potatoes are ideal for steaming and eating warm with summer salads or cold and tossed in mayonnaise for potato salad. Maincrop potatoes make the best roast, chipped or jacket potatoes.

Radishes

Radishes are a wonderful crop for beginners and children to grow because they are so quick to mature: they can be harvested in as little as four weeks. You will be familiar with the red globe radishes most commonly sold in supermarkets, but other varieties are white, pink, pointed or cylindrical with varying amounts of pepperiness.

Growing

> **Sowing:** Sow radishes *in situ* in fertile, moisture-retentive soil. You can plant seeds successively from spring to autumn. Make sure the soil is moist. Select a shadier spot for summer planting.

> **Varieties:** 'French Breakfast' is one of the fastest growing varieties. 'Purple Plum' has crisp, white flesh.

> **Tending:** Ensure radishes are kept watered in hot weather otherwise they can become woody or bolt.

> **Container gardening:** Radishes of any variety are ideal for containers and window boxes.

Did You Know?

Most of the 'hot' taste of radishes is in the skin; peel them for a milder flavour.

Protecting

> **Pests:** Cover the radishes with horticultural fleece to protect against flea beetle. Slugs can be a problem; deter them with barriers or traps.

> **Diseases:** Occasionally, radishes get cabbage root fly; this can be prevented with horticultural fleece.

Harvesting and Storing

> **Harvesting:** Harvest radishes when they are small and tender. Larger radishes can get tough and too peppery. Radishes do not last well in the ground so harvest frequently.

> **Storage:** Radishes will store in the fridge for a few days, but it is better to sow every week or so for a successional, fresh crop. Cut off the tops and store in an airtight container.

Herbs

Herbs make a wonderful addition to the garden and many are easy to grow. There are many herbs and your favourites will depend on your own taste. This section covers some of the more popular and easy-to-grow annual and perennial herbs.

Basil

Basil needs a lot of sun and grows well on a sunny windowsill. You can grow it outdoors, as long as you have a hot, sunny summer. Basil is a valuable companion plant as its scent helps deter pests.

Did You Know?

In Mediterranean countries, people believe that eating basil with the evening meal promotes sound sleep.

Growing

▶ **Sowing:** Sow seeds directly into rich, moist, freely draining soil. It needs full sun and is best started in a greenhouse or inside. Transplant it in the early summer when the soil and air temperatures have warmed up, or plant into containers on your patio.

▶ **Varieties:** There are many varieties of basil. The one you are most likely to see has dark glossy green leaves, but you can get red basil too, as well as varieties with different-shaped leaves.

▶ **Tending:** Basil is easy to take care of. If it is in a pot and the weather is hot, it may require daily watering; keep an eye on it and let the plant tell you when it needs more water. You can allow it to just wilt before watering it again, which will help to prevent over-watering.

245

▶ **Container gardening:** 'Genovese' is large leafed and used in Italian cooking. 'Greek' basil makes an excellent pot plant with its tiny leaves. 'Purple Ruffles' is an intriguing-looking basil with purple, almost black leaves.

Protecting

▶ **Pests:** Slugs may eat basil; deter them with barriers or set traps.

Harvesting and Storing

▶ **Harvesting:** If you keep pinching out the tips and take off flowers before they form you should be rewarded with a long harvest. Pick the leaves as soon as you like – more will soon grow!

▶ **Storage:** Select the leaves you want and use them straight away or cut stems and store them in a glass of water for a few days. Basil can be frozen or dried.

Eating

Basil is a versatile herb that lends itself to Mediterranean cooking. You can eat a few small leaves with salad. Basil is the perfect herb to serve with tomatoes and is the main ingredient of pesto. You can add basil to summer casseroles and soups and it blends well with tomatoes in a pasta sauce.

Mint

Mint is called a weed in many people's gardens. It is simple to grow, but make sure you contain the roots in pots. There are many types of mint: the most common are peppermint and spearmint, but you can also grow apple mint, lemon mint, ginger mint and even chocolate mint! It is nearly impossible to kill mint, so pests and diseases are not a problem.

Growing

▶ **Sowing:** Once you plant mint it's there for life, so choose your site wisely. Contain it in pots to prevent it becoming invasive. You can sow seeds or take a cutting from a friend; just pop the cutting in soil and it will take root effortlessly. Mint is not fussy about soil type and will withstand some shade. You can grow mint in pots indoors during the winter.

▶ **Varieties:** There are many varieties to choose from: spearmint is the most common mint and makes the best mint tea; chocolate mint is great if you want something a bit different.

▶ **Tending:** Mint likes to be kept moist and will do well in a slightly shady spot.

▶ **Container gardening:** Mint is especially suited to pots.

Top Tip

Mint eases congestion; if you're stuffed up with a cold, make a cup of mint tea and inhale the vapours as you drink.

Harvesting and Storing

▶ **Harvesting:** Harvest mint regularly; the more you cut it, the more it will grow. Remove the flowering heads so that the plant produces more leaves.

▶ **Storage:** Cut stems of mint and store in a glass of water for a few days. For long-term storage, dry or freeze it.

247

Eating

Mint is refreshing and uplifting. You can chop it finely and add to salads; tabbouleh is one recipe that calls for a lot of mint. Mint is the traditional accompaniment to roast lamb – finely chop and mix into vinegar for mint sauce. You can seep two fresh leaves in a cup of water for mint tea and mix it into butter as the perfect topping for new potatoes.

Parsley

You'll find both flat-leafed and curly parsley. Both can be grown outdoors, although you may have more success on a windowsill.

Growing

▶ **Sowing:** Parsley can be difficult to germinate. You can help by soaking the seeds in lukewarm water for a couple of hours before sowing. Sow in moist compost in pots or outdoors in a damp, semi-shaded or sunny position. Parsley needs rich, moist soil and pots of compost are ideal. Sow successionally from spring for a continuous supply.

▶ **Varieties:** Try the flat-leaf 'Italian Plain Leaf' or the curly 'Champion Moss Curled'.

▶ **Tending:** Keep parsley moist; it will not survive if it dries out.

▶ **Container gardening:** Parsley is perfect for patio containers or window boxes.

Did You Know?

Because parsley seeds take so long to germinate, it was once believed that they travelled to the devil and back before sprouting.

Harvesting and Storing

▶ **Harvesting:** Pick leaves regularly for an increased supply.

▶ **Storage:** Store cut stems in a glass of water for a few days. Parsley can be frozen or dried.

Protecting

Parsley is fairly disease-free. The only pest you may encounter is parsley worm – the two-inch long larvae of the black swallowtail butterfly – dispose of this before it strips down your plant.

Eating

Parsley sauce is traditionally served with fish: make a béchamel sauce and add a handful of chopped fresh parsley. It makes a delicate addition to salads and combines well with all vegetables. Parsley can be substituted for watercress to make an iron-rich soup.

Thyme

Thyme is a low-growing herb with pretty white or pink flowers. It will withstand most treatment except very wet soils. You can use thyme as an attractive and useful ground cover – if left to flower it will attract beneficial insects. Thyme does really well in poor soils and will grow in wall cracks and between paving slabs.

Growing

▶ **Sowing:** Thyme likes full sun but will tolerate a bit of shade. Its most important requirement is free-draining soil. Sow seeds *in situ* when the weather is warm enough.

▶ **Varieties:** There are many different varieties of thyme; try lemon thyme for a different flavour.

▶ **Tending:** Like sage, thyme can become straggly and woody after a few years. Each year, take some cuttings and replant them so that you have a continuous supply of fresh, tender leaves. It will withstand all but the harshest winters and still provide you with green leaves.

▶ **Container gardening:** Thyme is ideal for containers, including pots, hanging baskets and window boxes.

Protecting

▶ **Pests:** Keep an eye out for ants – there is a risk of them making their nests around the roots and thus causing disruption.

▶ **Diseases:** Damp and humid conditions can cause mould and rot.

Harvesting and Storing

▶ **Harvesting:** Pick off short stems with the amount of thyme you want to use in your meal. Just before the flowers appear you can cut the bush right down and it will grow again.

▶ **Storage:** Thyme will survive winter, so pick leaves as you need them. You can also freeze or dry them.

Eating

Thyme is traditionally served with meat and poultry dishes. You can steep a short stem of leaves in a cup of water for thyme tea, which is great as a winter tonic when there are infections around. A few snipped leaves are good in salads, but don't overdo it as the flavour is quite strong. Thyme is used to add flavour to stocks and soups.

Checklist

Members of the cabbage family such as brussels sprouts, winter cabbages and kale are good choicesif you have alkaline soil. They give a steady supply of food throughout the winter.

▶ If you want to improve the nitrogen content of your soil, try growing legumes such as peas and beans.

▶ If you are looking for prolific vegetable yields then runner beans, courgettes and potatoes are excellent choices. Keep up with the picking and harvesting or the plants will stop producing new vegetables.

▶ Try growing vegetables which will complement each other; sweetcorn, beans and squash are a good example as the sweetcorn plants act as poles for the beans to climb whilst beans fix nitrogen in the soil and squash suppresses weeds.

▶ If you want to grow something with a quick return, salad leaves are the best choice and can be ready in weeks. They are also well suited to being grown in containers.

▶ Protect your vegetables from slugs using barriers and traps. This is very important with young plants.

▶ If space is at a premium in your garden then you may like to try growing vegetables such as cucumbers, courgettes, pumpkins and squashes in a vertical fashion as they require a lot of ground space if grown traditionally.

▶ As long as you have well-drained soil then garlic, onions and shallots make an easy choice for those new to growing vegetables. Simply push the bulbs into the ground and surround with mulch.

▶ Aubergines, peppers and tomatoes need warm conditions to grow well so are ideal if you have a greenhouse. These vegetables are often expensive to buy, so growing them is a great money saver.

▶ Herbs are perfectly suited to growing in pots or window boxes. They often need sheltered and warm conditions so you may even wish to grow them indoors.

Further Reading

Berry, S., *Kitchen Harvest: A Cook's Guide to Growing Organic Fruit, Vegetables and Herbs in Containers*, Frances Lincoln, 2004

Clevely, A. M., *The Allotment Book*, Collins, 2008

Courtier, J., *The Complete Vegetable Gardener: A Practical Guide to Growing Fresh and Delicious Vegetables*, Reader's Digest, 2006

Diacono, M., *Veg Patch: River Cottage Handbook No. 4*, Bloomsbury Publishing Plc, 2009

Dowding, C., *Organic Gardening: The Natural No-dig Way*, Green Books, 2007

Grigson, S., *The Vegetable Bible: The Definitive Guide*, Collins, 2009

Guerra, M., Klein, C. and Whitefield P., *The Edible Container Garden: Fresh Food from Tiny Places*, Gaia Books Ltd, 2005

Halstead, A. and Greenwood, P., *RHS Pests and Diseases*, Dorling Kindersley, 2009

Hamlyn All Colour Gardening: 200 Veg Growing Basics, Hamlyn, 2009

Hessyayon, D. G., *The Green Garden Expert*, Expert, 2009

Hobson, J. C. J. and Rant, P., *Successful Smallholding: Planning, Starting and Managing Your Enterprise*, The Crowood Press Ltd, 2009

Howard, Sir A., *Farming and Gardening for Health or Disease*, Soil Association Ltd, 2006

Klein, C. and the Royal Horticultural Society (RHS), *Grow Your Own Veg*, Mitchell Beazley, 2007

Larkcom, J., *Grow Your Own Vegetables*, Frances Lincoln, 2002

Mabey, R., *Food for Free*, Collins, 2004

Ott, S., Rawlings, E. and Warwick, R., *Grow Your Own Fruit and Veg in Plot, Pots or Growbags: The A-Z Guide to Growing and Cooking Farm-fresh Food*, Foulsham, 2008

Purnell, B., *Crops in Pots: 50 Great Container Projects Using Vegetables, Fruit and Herbs*, Hamlyn, 2007

Seymour, J., Sutherland W. and Schumacher, E. F., *The New Complete Book of Self-sufficiency: The Classic Guide for Realists and Dreamers*, Dorling Kindersley, 2003

Strauss, R., *Green Guides: Compost*, Flame Tree Publishing, 2009

Swithinbank, A., *The Greenhouse Gardener*, Frances Lincoln, 2006

Titchmarsh, Alan, *The Kitchen Gardener: Grow Your Own Fruit and Veg*, BBC Books, 2008

Vegetables in a Small Garden: Simple Steps to Success (RHS), Dorling Kindersley, 2007

Warren, P., *How to Store Your Own Garden Produce: The Key to Self-sufficiency*, Green Books, 2008

Wong, J., *How to Grow Your Own Drugs: Easy Recipes for Natural Remedies and Beauty Treats*, Collins, 2009

Magazines

Grow Your Own magazine, Aceville Publications, Tel: 0844 815 0030, www.growfruitandveg.co.uk

Kitchen Garden magazine, Mortons Media Group, Tel: 01507 529529, www.kitchengarden.co.uk

Websites

www.allotment.org.uk
A great site for allotment enthusiasts, imparting helpful advice and allotment-based recipes.

www.applegategardens.co.uk
A garden design service offering bespoke garden designs as well as DIY landscaping suggestions.

www.backyardgardener.com
A cornucopia of growing tips, the site also includes a comprehensive gardening dictionary and green-themed poetry section.

www.bbc.co.uk/digin
The BBC's online campaign encourages domestic vegetable cultivation and cooking in a fun, accessible manner.

www.bbc.co.uk/gardenersworld
Fans of the long-serving television show can revisit clips and discover a range of supplementary gardening information.

www.bbc.co.uk/gardening/basics/techniques/
The BBC's gardening homepage provides basic growing techniques for the budding gardener.

www.davesgarden.com
Established "for gardeners, by gardeners," the site provides handy tips and helpful hints from its members, along with a list of approved online product websites.

www.gardenguides.com
A detailed plant directory is accompanied by an invaluable pest-management section.

www.gardenorganic.org.uk
Garden Organic is a national charity promoting organic gardening and food.

www.growingtaste.com
A useful resource for growers particularly keen to maximize the flavour of their vegetable crop.

www.kitchengardeners.org
Hosting a series of links to individual growing and cookery blogs, the site supports a global gardening community.

landshare.channel4.com
Channel 4's Landshare programme offers an effective way for participating landowners to contact growers looking for space to satisfy their green fingers.

www.nickys-nursery.co.uk
Nicky's Nursery provides a catalogue of great value seed packets, complemented by a helpful vegetable sowing calendar.

www.rhs.org.uk
Royal Horticultural Society website offering an extensive range of gardening advice, from cultivation to pest control, as well as a forum allowing you to post personal tips and have your queries answered.

www.unwins.co.uk
Unwins is a valuable online supplier of vegetable seeds, all carefully selected and picked by hand.

www.vegetableexpert.co.uk
Contains lots of articles providing advice on nutrition and buying, cooking and storing vegetables as well as growing them.

www.veggiegardeningtips.com
Offers organic growing techniques and recommended gardening products in a personal and approachable style.

Index